teach® yourself

beginner's
german

rosi mcnab

advisory editor

paul coggle

Launched in 1938, the **teach yourself** series grew rapidly in response to the world's wartime needs. Loved and trusted by over 50 million readers, the series has continued to respond to society's changing interests and passions and now, 70 years on, includes over 500 titles, from Arabic and Beekeeping to Yoga and Zulu. What would you like to learn?

be where you want to be with **teach yourself**

For UK order enquiries: please contact Bookpoint Ltd, 130 Milton Park, Abingdon, Oxon, OX14 4SB. Telephone: +44 (0) 1235 827720. Fax. +44 (0) 1235 400454. Lines are open 09.00–17.00, Monday to Saturday, with a 24-hour message answering service. Details about our titles and how to order are available at www.teachyourself.co.uk

For USA order enquiries: please contact McGraw-Hill Customer Services, PO Box 545, Blacklick, OH 43004-0545, USA. Telephone: 1-800-722-4726. Fax: 1-614-755-5645.

For Canada order enquiries: please contact McGraw-Hill Ryerson Ltd, 300 Water St, Whitby, Ontario, L1N 9B6, Canada. Telephone: 905 430 5000. Fax: 905 430 5020.

Long renowned as the authoritative source for self-guided learning – with more than 50 million copies sold worldwide – the **teach yourself** series includes over 500 titles in the fields of languages, crafts, hobbies, business, computing and education.

British Library Cataloguing in Publication Data: a catalogue record for this title is available from the British Library.

Library of Congress Catalog Card Number: on file.

First published in UK 1992 by Hodder Education, part of Hachette Livre UK, 338 Euston Road, London, NW1 3BH.

First published in US 1992 by The McGraw-Hill Companies, Inc.

This edition published 2008.

The **teach yourself** name is a registered trade mark of Hodder Headline.

Copyright © 1992, 2003, 2008 Rosi McNab

Typeset by Transet Limited, Coventry, England.
Printed in Great Britain for Hodder Education, an Hachette Livre UK Company, 338 Euston Road, London NW1 3BH, by CPI Cox and Wyman, Reading, Berkshire, RG1 8EX.

The publisher has used its best endeavours to ensure that the URLs for external websites referred to in this book are correct and active at the time of going to press. However, the publisher and the author have no responsibility for the websites and can make no guarantee that a site will remain live or that the content will remain relevant, decent or appropriate.

Hachette Livre UK's policy is to use papers that are natural, renewable and recyclable products and made from wood grown in sustainable forests. The logging and manufacturing processes are expected to conform to the environmental regulations of the country of origin.

Impression number   10 9 8 7 6 5 4 3 2 1
Year   2012 2011 2010 2009 2008

iii

contents

introduction

The guidelines given in this introduction are intended to provide some useful advice on studying alone and on how to make the most of the course.

If you have the recording, make sure you have your CD player nearby when you are working as you should use it to listen to the dialogues and the exercises. If you don't have a CD player, use the **Pronunciation notes** to help you pronounce the words properly. You should always *read the words and the dialogues out loud*. This will give you confidence to use them when called upon to do so in a real situation.

People learn in different ways: some like to learn rules, a very few find it easy to learn by heart, some like to learn by writing things down and others prefer to learn by association. Try different methods until you find which works best for you.

How the units work

Within each unit you will find the following components:

Dialogues

As you get more confident you should try covering up one side of the dialogue and see if you can still remember what to say. All the dialogues are also on the recording. You should practise saying them with the recording.

Vocabulary boxes

These contain **keywords** – words (and phrases) which will help you to understand the text. Practise saying them out loud. Try different ways to help you remember their meaning. Here are some ways you might find helpful:

- Cover up the English and see if you can remember what the words mean.
- Cover up the German and see if you can remember the German words. You will find this much more difficult.
- Write down the first letter of each word and see how many you can remember.
- Choose five new words or expressions and try to learn them.
- Count how many words there are and see how many you can recall. See if you can think of English words which sound similar, e.g.

  Hund – *(hound) dog;*
  Blume – *(bloom) flower*

Exercises

The various exercises provide practice in the German that you have learned in each unit. It is important to make good use of them so that you can be sure of understanding and remembering the language in one unit before you go on to the next.

The answers to the exercises are given at the back on pages 210–17.

Listening exercises

You will need to use the recording for these.

Pronunciation notes

These notes will help you with the pronunciation of new words. However, don't forget to also make good use of the full **Pronunciation guide** given at the end of this **Introduction**.

In the early units a phonetic version of the sound of words is given in square brackets for new words in the word lists.

Language notes

These are notes about the language, useful expressions and hints about when to use them.

Word patterns

All languages behave according to certain patterns and rules. This section helps you by providing models of the patterns of the language. When you have got used to one pattern you can often make lots of new expressions simply by changing a word or part of a word.

Revision

At the end of each of Units 1–10 is a revision and consolidation section.

Note on Unit 11

Unit 11 is a reference unit on German verbs and does not work like the other units. Although it includes some exercises, there are no dialogues. It is not necessary to learn all the material in Unit 11 at once, but it includes information to which you will need to refer as you continue with the second half of the course.

Symbols

▶ This indicates that the recording is needed for the following section.

ℹ This indicates a section giving information about the customs and way of life of the German-speaking countries.

Pronunciation guide

A few tips to help you acquire an authentic accent:
- Always say everything out loud, preferably as if you were talking to someone on the other side of the room!
- Whenever possible get someone to say the dialogues with you. Listen carefully to the recording, or if possible ask a native speaker to read some of the words for you.
- Record your voice and compare it with the recording.
- Ask a native speaker to listen to your pronunciation and tell you how to improve it.
- Make a list of words that give you trouble and practise them.

▶ And now practise saying these place names:

Köln Bonn Berlin München Wien Zürich Düsseldorf
Frankfurt Hamburg Hannover Leipzig Halle Freiburg Basel

[curl-n] [bon] [bairleen] [m*in-chen] [veen] [ts*irich]
[d*isseldoorf] [frank-furt] [ham-burg] [hano-fer] [l-eye-pt-
sich] [hal-uh] [fry-boorg] [bah-zel]

* ü sounds as if you were trying to say **u** but actually say **i**!

German sounds

Most English speakers have little difficulty in pronouncing the
German sounds because the two languages share some of their
linguistic roots and they both belong to the same family of
languages. Many German words are spoken aloud as they are
spelt.

▶ The consonants

Most of these sounds are the same as in English spoken in the
south of England. The ones which are not have asterisks:

b	as in *bath*	Bad
c	as in *camping*	Campingplatz
d	as in *dark*	dunkel
f	as in *free*	frei
g	as in *garden*	Garten
h	as in *hard*	hart
*j	as *y* in *yes*	ja
k	as in *climb*	klettern
l	as in *last*	letzte
m	as in *man*	Mann
n	as in *night*	Nacht
p	as in *place*	Platz
*qu	as *kv* in *Kvetch*	Qualität (*quality*)
r	produced at the back of the throat	rot
*s	as *z* in *zone*	Sohn (son)
t	as in *tea*	Tee
*v	as *f* in *follow*	Volkswagen (**folksvaagen**)
*w	as *v* in *van*	Wecker (*alarm clock*)
x	as in *fax*	Fax

y	as y in *yen*	Yen
*z	as *ts* in *tsetse*	Zeitung
		(*newspaper*)

[In Southern Germany, the 'r' is trilled.]

▶ The vowels

The vowels have a long and short form.

The short form is normally used when followed by two or more consonants and the long form when followed by one consonant, or h + one consonant.

The short form is given first:

a as *a*	in *cat*	Katze
	father	Vater
e as *e*	in *bed*	Bett
ay	*day*	Tee (*tea*)
i as *i*	in *pit*	mit (*with*)
	kilo	Kilo
o as *o*	in *not*	noch (*yet*)
	home	ohne (*without*)
u as *u*	in *butcher*	Bus
oe	*shoe*	Schuh
		Guten Tag! (*good day*)

▶ Special letters and sounds

1 It is difficult to represent these sounds in English. If possible you should listen to the recording and practise them after it:

ä   ö   ü

¨ is called an 'Umlaut' and is used on an **a**, **o** or **u**. It changes the sound of the word.

The short form is given first:

ä sounds	*eh*	Mädchen (*girl*)
	ay	spät (*late*)
ö sounds	*uh*	wöchentlich (*weekly*)
	er	schön (*pretty*)
ü sounds	*i*	fünf (*five*)
	u	Bücher (*books*), Tür (*door*)

2 ß represents 'ss' and is used after a long vowel:
Straße (*street*), Fuß (*foot*)

3   **ch** is pronounced as *ch* in the Scottish word *loch*
ich (*I*) Bu<u>ch</u> (*book*)

4   **au** is pronounced *ow* as in *owl* Fr<u>au</u> (*Mrs*)
<u>Au</u>f Wiedersehen! (*goodbye*)
äu is pronounced *oy* as in *coy* Fr<u>äu</u>lein (*Miss*)

5   At the end of a word:

b	is pronounced *p*	hal<u>b</u> (*half*)
d	is pronounced *t*	Hun<u>d</u> (*dog*)
g	is pronounced *k*	Ta<u>g</u> (*day*)
ig	is pronounced *'ch*	fert<u>ig</u> (*ready*)
s	is pronounced *s* (not *z*)	Hau<u>s</u> (*house*)

6   **ei** is pronounced   *eye*   dr<u>ei</u> (*three*), W<u>ei</u>n (*wine*)
ie is pronounced   *ee*   v<u>ie</u>r (*four*), B<u>ie</u>r (*beer*)

7   **sch** is pronounced   *sh* as in   <u>Sch</u>uh (*shoe*)
sp is pronounced   *shp* as in   <u>sp</u>ät   (*late*)
st is pronounced   *sht* as in   <u>St</u>adt (*town*)

8   **e** at the end of a word is pronounced *-uh*:
Bitt<u>e</u> (*please*) Dank<u>e</u> (*thank you*)

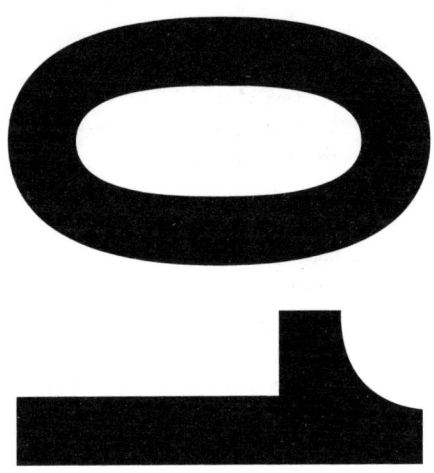

01

guten Tag!
good day!

In this unit you will learn how to
- say 'hello' and 'goodbye'
- greet and address someone
- ask to speak to someone
- say you don't understand
- ask if anyone speaks English

Before you start

Read the introduction to the course on page vii. This gives some useful advice on studying alone and on how to make the most of the course.

If you have the recording, make sure you have it handy as you'll be using it when you work with the **Dialogues** and the **Pronunciation notes**. If you don't have the recording, use the **Pronunciation guide** on page ix to help you with the pronunciation of new words and phrases.

Remember that studying for 20 minutes regularly is more effective than spending two hours at one session every so often. To help yourself to use this course as effectively as possible, follow this study guide (and adapt it to suit your own learning patterns as you go along, if you wish):

1 Listen to or read the **Dialogues** once or twice (listen without the book first of all, if you have the recording).
2 Go over each one bit by bit in conjunction with the **Key words**. Do the same for each of the **Key words** that has no accompanying dialogue.
3 Use the **Learning notes** to help the material in the **Key words** to sink in.
4 Study the **Language notes** and **Word patterns** as these give you information that you will use over and over again later.
5 Do the **Exercises** and the **Revision** if there is one at the end of the unit; check your answers in the **Key to the exercises** at the end of the book. Only start a new unit when you are sure of all the material in the previous one.

Can you think of any German words that you already know, such as the words for 'hello' and 'thank you?' Say them out loud and then check them in the **Key words** below.

▶ Guten Tag, Herr Braun! *Good day, Mr Brown!*

Herr [hair]	*Mr*
Frau [fr-ow]	*Mrs*
gut [goot]	*good/well*
danke [dankuh]	*thanks*
guten Tag [gooten tahk]	*good day*

Wie geht es Ihnen?	*How are you?*
[vee gate es ee-nen]	
Es geht mir gut.	*I am well.* (lit. *It goes to me*
[es gate meer goot]	*well*)
auf Wiedersehen	*goodbye*
[ow-uf veeder-say-un]	
auch [ow-uch]	*also*

Hallo and **hi** are both used as informal greetings.

Learning notes

- Read the words and expressions out loud. Concentrate on the pronunciation.
- If you have the recording listen to the words and repeat them after the recording.
- Cover up the meaning and see how many you can remember. Listen again and think of what the words mean as you hear them.
- Cover up the German words and see if you can remember them.

▶ Dialogue 1

Frau Taylor

Guten Tag, Herr Braun.
[gooten tahk hair brown]

Herr Braun

Guten Tag, Frau Taylor.

Wie geht es Ihnen?
[vee gate es ee-nen?]

Danke, es geht mir gut,
und Ihnen?
[dankuh, es gate meer goot,
unt ee-nen?]

Auch gut, danke.
[ow-uch goot dankuh]
Auf Wiedersehen, Herr
Braun!
[ow-uf veeder-say-un]

Auf Wiedersehen, Frau
Taylor!

Learning notes

- Imagine that you are Mrs Taylor. Cover up the left-hand side of the dialogue. Greet Herr Braun, answer his question and complete the conversation.
- Now cover up the right-hand side and practise Herr Braun's part of the conversation.

Exercise 1

How do you say the following?

a good day	**d** goodbye	**g** thank you
b also	**e** well	**h** how are you?
c Mr	**f** I'm well	**i** and

▶ Guten Tag, Frau Meyer! *Good day, Mrs Meyer!*

In the first dialogue you were talking to a man. In this dialogue you learn how to address a woman.

Guten Morgen! [gooten more-ghen]	*Good morning!*
Tschüs or Tschüss [tshewss]	*bye*
Guten Abend! [gooten ah-bend]	*Good evening!*
Gute Nacht! [gootuh nacht]	*Good night!*
ich bin [ich bin]	*I am*
nicht so gut [nicht so goot]	*not so well*

Das tut mir Leid.	*I'm sorry.*
[das toot meer lite]	
Angenehm!	*Pleased to meet you!*
[anger-name]	(lit: *pleasant/nice*)
Ich habe Kopfschmerzen.	*I have a headache.*
[ich habuh kopf-schmairtsen]	

Pronunciation tip

Remember **ch** as in **loch**.

Learning notes

- Practise saying the words (after the recording if you have it).
- Cover up the English words and see if you can remember what the German words mean.
- Cover up the German words and see if you can remember them.

ℹ Germans use 'Frau' when addressing a young woman of about 18 or more whether she is married or not. They tend to be formal and will usually shake hands when meeting you or saying goodbye and add your name to the greeting:

As a general rule you use:

Guten Morgen first thing in the morning,
Guten Tag after about 10am,
Guten Abend after 5pm and
Gute Nacht when you are going to bed.

Tschüss, Tschüssi *'bye* are widely used in informal situations.
Servus, Ade *'bye* are both used informally in South Germany.

▶ Dialogue 2

Mr Smith	**Frau Meyer**
Guten Tag, Frau Meyer!	
Ich bin Martin Smith.	
	Guten Tag, Herr Smith!
	Angenehm.
	Wie geht es Ihnen?

Danke, gut, und Ihnen?

> Nicht so gut.
> Ich habe Kopfschmerzen.

Das tut mir Leid.
Auf Wiedersehen, Frau
Meyer.

> Auf Wiedersehen, Herr
> Smith.

Practise the same dialogue for use: **a** early in the morning; and **b** in the evening.

Exercise 2

Welches Wort fehlt? *Which word is missing?*

a Es ... mir gut.

c Das tut ... Leid.

b Ich ... Martin Smith.

d Auf ...., Frau Meyer.

▶ Listening exercise 1

Listen to these people and work out what time of day it is:

i early morning

iii late afternoon

ii later morning

iv night time

Now listen again and add if they are addressing (a) a man, (b) a woman or (c) a young woman.

 In South Germany and Austria people often say:

Grüß Gott!   *Good day!*
[grewss got]   (lit: greet God)

▶ Verzeihung *Excuse me, please*

You have learned how to greet someone you know or to whom you have been introduced. The next dialogue teaches you how to ask for someone and say you don't understand.

Verzeihung. [fair-tseye-hoong]	*Pardon/Excuse me, please.*
Sind Sie ...? [zindt zee ...?]	*Are you ...?*
Mein Name ist ... [mine nahm-uh ist ...]	*My name is ...*
Wie bitte? [vee bittuh?]	*Pardon?*
Ich heiße ... [ich high-suh ...]	*I am called ...*
Wie heißen Sie? [vee high-sen zee?]	*What is your name?*
Ich verstehe nicht. [ich fair-shtayuh nicht]	*I don't understand.*
Er ist nicht da. [air ist nicht daa]	*He is not here.*
heute [hoy-tuh]	*today*
Sprechen Sie Englisch? [shprech-un zee ehng-lish?]	*Do you speak English?*
Ich verstehe ein bisschen. [ich fairshtay-uh 'ine biss-schun]	*I understand a bit.*
Wann kann ich ihn sehen? [van can ich een zay-un?]	*When can I see him?*
morgen [more-gun]	*tomorrow*
Vielen Dank. [feel-un dank]	*Many thanks.*

Pronunciation tips

ei sounds **aye**   ie sounds **ee**

v sounds **f** – remember **Volkswagen** is pronounced 'folksvaagen'.

Learning notes

- Read the words/phrases out loud and concentrate on the pronunciation.
- Read or *listen* again and think of the meaning.
- Cover up the German words and see how many you can remember.
- How do you say: *I don't understand. Do you speak English?*

▶ Dialogue 3

Mr Smith	Herr Kryschinski
Verzeihung, sind Sie Herr Schulz?	
	Nein. Mein Name ist Kryschinski.
Wie bitte?	
	Ich heiße Kryschinski. Wie heißen Sie?
Smith.	
	Angenehm. Herr Schulz ist heute nicht da.
Ich verstehe nicht.	
	Herr Schulz ist nicht da.
Sprechen Sie Englisch?	
	Ich verstehe ein bisschen. Mr Schulz is not here.
Wann kann ich ihn sehen?	
	Morgen.
Vielen Dank. Auf Wiedersehen.	
	Auf Wiedersehen, Herr Smith.

Learning note

- Read the dialogue out loud and then cover up the different sides in turn and see how much you can remember.

Exercise 3

Wie sagt man das auf Deutsch? *How do you say it in German?*

a What is your name?
b I don't understand
c I am called …
d Excuse me, please.
e tomorrow

f Herr Schulz is not here.
g goodbye
h Pardon?
i a bit

Revision

1 What greeting would you use at these times?

| **08:30** | **11:15** | **14:30** | **18:15** |
| a | b | c | d |

2 Imagine you are staying in a hotel in Germany and Frau Hoffmann calls for you at 6pm. What would you say to her?

a Guten   b Guten   c Guten   d Gute
  Morgen   Tag   Abend   Nacht

3 During the evening she says:

Es geht mir nicht gut. What would you say?

a Vielen Dank b Auf Wiedersehen c Das tut mir Leid

4 How do you pronounce these words and phrases?

> **i** Wie geht es Ihnen? **ii** und **iii** Danke
> **iv** Herr **v** Frau **vi** auch **vii** Auf Wiedersehen

5 Welches Wort fehlt? *Which word is missing?*

a Sind ... Herr Braun?   e Wie ...... Sie?
b Wie ......?   f Er ist ..... da.
c Ich .... nicht.   g .... Wiedersehen.
d Ich ..... Fred.   h Ich verstehe ein ....

6 Welche Antwort passt? *Which is the right answer?*

a Wie heißen Sie?   i Ja, ein bisschen.
b Sprechen Sie Englisch?   ii Mein Name ist ...
c Wie geht es Ihnen?   iii Nein, ich bin ...
d Sind Sie Herr Brown?   iv Gut, danke und Ihnen?

▶ Listening exercise 2

Check you can understand which is the right answer: i, ii or iii?

a The speaker says **i** good morning **ii** good day **iii** good evening.
b S/he is called **i** Fräulein Schmidt **ii** Herr Schmidt **iii** Frau Schmidt.

c S/he **i** speaks English **ii** speaks some English **iii** doesn't speak English.

d S/he **i** says s/he is not well **ii** says s/he is very well **iii** asks if you are well.

Sign language

How many of the signs do you know already?

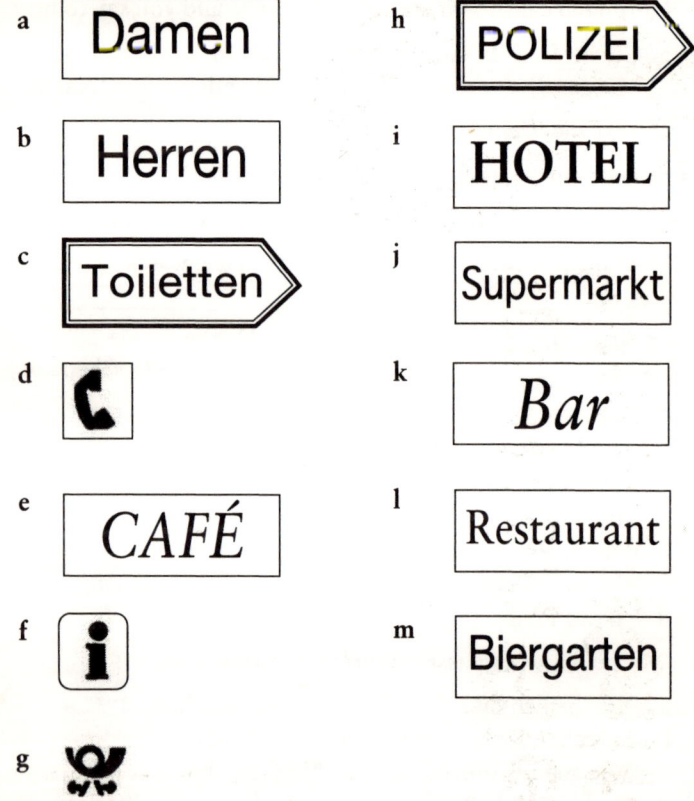

a Damen

b Herren

c Toiletten

d ☏

e *CAFÉ*

f ℹ

g

h POLIZEI

i HOTEL

j Supermarkt

k *Bar*

l Restaurant

m Biergarten

Congratulations! You have now completed the first unit.

02

trinken Sie eine Tasse Kaffee?

would you like a cup of coffee?

In this unit you will learn how to
- say 'please' and 'thank you'
- say what you would like to drink
- ask someone what they would like to drink
- ask for a drink at a café
- ask for the bill

▶ Kaffee und Kuchen *Coffee and cakes*

This box includes the words you need for the first dialogue:

Trinken Sie ...? [trink-en zee]	*Would you like (to drink) ...?* (lit. *drink you ...?*)
eine Tasse Kaffee [eye-nuh tass-uh café]	*a cup of coffee*
Ja, gerne. [yah, gair-nuh]	*Yes, I would like to* (lit *yes, willingly*)
mit [mitt]	*with*
ohne [oh-nuh]	*without*
Milch und Zucker [milch unt tsook-uh]	*milk and sugar*
ein Stück Kuchen ['ine shtewk coo-chen]	*a piece of cake*
bitte schön [bitt-uh shurn]	*here you are*
bitte [bitt-uh]	*please*
Danke/Danke schön. [dank-uh/dank-uh-shurn]	*Thank you.*
Ich trinke keinen Kaffee. [ich trink-uh kine-uhn café]	*I don't drink coffee.*

Learning notes

- Say the words out loud (after the recording), concentrating on the pronunciation.
- Cover up the English and see if you can remember what all the German words and phrases mean.
- Cover up the German and see if you can remember it.

ℹ Saying 'please' and 'thank you'

If you thank someone in German they will reply **bitte**, which usually means *please* but in this case means *don't mention it*.

If someone says **danke** to you don't forget to reply **bitte**!

If someone offers you something and you say **danke** they will take it to mean *no thank you*. If you want it, say **bitte** instead. This is a mistake you are likely to make only once!

 Coffee

Germans tend to drink a lot of coffee, and they drink quite strong 'real' coffee in preference to instant coffee. It is usually served with cold milk or **Kaffeesahne** (cream for coffee – like evaporated milk) and white sugar (**Zucker**) or **Kandis** (crystallized sugar lumps).

If you want decaffeinated coffee you ask for **koffeinfrei** [coffaynfry], i.e. free of caffeine, or **entkoffeinierten Kaffee** (decaffeinated coffee). If you want artificial sweetener you ask for **Süßstoff**.

▶ Dialogue 4

You are visiting Herr Braun and are offered coffee and cakes after your journey.

Herr Braun	Sie (you)
	Guten Tag, Herr Braun. Wie geht es Ihnen?
Gut, danke und Ihnen?	
	Auch gut, danke.
Trinken Sie eine Tasse Kaffee?	
	Ja, gerne.
Mit Milch und Zucker?	
	Ohne Zucker.
Ein Stück Kuchen?	
	Ja, bitte.
Bitte schön.	
	Danke.
Bitte.	

Learning notes

- Read the dialogue out loud.
- Cover up your side of the conversation and see if you can say your part.
- Now imagine you are Herr Braun and cover up his part of the conversation and see if you can say it.

Wie trinken Sie Kaffee? *How do you like your coffee?*

a mit Milch
b mit Milch und Zucker
c mit Milch und ohne Zucker
d mit Zucker und ohne Milch
e Ich trinke keinen Kaffee.

▶ Ich trinke lieber Tee *I prefer tea*

In the first dialogue of this unit you were in Germany, now Herr Braun is visiting you. What are you going to offer him?

Wie war die Reise? [vee var dee rye-zuh?]	*How was the journey?*
Ich bin müde [ich bin mew-duh]	*I am tired.*
Ich trinke lieber ... [ich trink-uh lee-buh]	*I would prefer ...* (lit: *I drink rather ...*)
Tee [tay]	*tea*
oder [ode-uh]	*or*
Zitrone [tsit-rone-uh]	*lemon*
keinen Zucker [kine-en tsuckuh]	*no sugar*
Schokoladenkuchen [shock-o-lahd-uhn-koochen]	*chocolate cake*
Apfelsaft [app-fell-zaft]	*apple juice*
Orangensaft [or-ahnge-enn-zaft]	*orange juice* (**Orangensaft** is commonly shortened to **O-Saft**.)
Tomatensaft [toe-marten-zaft]	*tomato juice*
eine Dose [doze-uh]	*a can*
eine Flasche [flash-uh]	*a bottle*

Language notes

In German new words are often made by adding two (or more) words together. When you meet one of these long words look for the place where it divides and work out what the different parts mean, e.g.

Apfelkuchen	= Apfel	+ Kuchen
	= *apple*	*cake*
Biergarten	= Bier	+ Garten
	= *beer*	*garden*

Learning notes

- Say the words out loud (after the recording).
- Cover up the English and check you know what they mean.
- Now cover the German and see if you can say the German words.

Exercise 1

Was trinken Sie? *What are you drinking?*

a   b   c

d   e

Alkoholfreie Getränke *Non-alcoholic drinks*

f   g   h

i   j

▶ Dialogue 5

Sie	Herr Braun
Hallo, Herr Braun. Wie geht es Ihnen?	
	Gut, danke und Ihnen?
Wie war die Reise?	
	Nicht so gut, ich bin müde.
Trinken Sie eine Tasse Kaffee?	
	Ich trinke lieber Tee.
Mit Milch oder mit Zitrone?	
	Mit Milch.
Und Zucker?	
	Nein. Kein' Zucker.*
Ein Stück Schokoladenkuchen?	
	Gerne.
Bitte schön.	
	Danke.
Bitte.	

*The correct form is **keinen Zucker** but most people miss off the -en when they are speaking.

Learning notes

- Practise both sides of the conversation.
- Think about what the words and phrases mean as you say them.
- Remember you must say them out loud.

Exercise 2

What do these mean? Use the breakdown process explained under **Language notes** to work out what they are:

a Reisebüro
b Reiseschecks
c Reisekosten
d Zitronentee

▶ Im Café *In the café*

Was darf es sein?	*What can I get you?*
[vas darf es zine?]	(lit: *What may it be?*)
Ich möchte ... [ich merch-tuh]	*I would like ...*
Haben Sie ...? [hah-bun zee?]	*Have you ...?*
zu süß [tsoo zew-ss]	*too sweet*
zu trocken [tsoo trock-en]	*too dry*
halbtrocken [halp-trock-en]	*medium* (lit: *half-dry*)
ein Glas Wein ['ine glass vine]	*a glass of wine*
zwei Gläser Wein	*two glasses of wine*
[tsv-eye glazer vine]	
ein Glas Bier ['ine glass beer]	*a glass of beer*
Zahlen, bitte. [tsah-len]	*The bill, please.* (lit: *to pay*)
rot/weiß [rote/vice]	*red/white*
Das macht 5 (fünf) Euro.	*That is 5 Euros.* (lit: *That*
[das macht finf ow-ro]	*makes 5 Euros*)
Ich trinke keinen Alkohol.	*I don't drink alcohol.*
[al-coe-holl]	

ℹ️ Most German wine is white.

The best known are probably the Rhine wines (**Rheinwein**) such as:

Liebfraumilch – sold in a brown bottle.

Moselwein – from the vineyards on the banks of the river Moselle/or Mosel – sold in a green bottle.

Frankenwein – which comes from **Franken** or Franconia (a region in Northern Bavaria) – sold in a green bottle shaped like a bulb.

Terms of reference:

Tafelwein – is table wine.

Qualitätswein – is a quality wine.

Qualitätswein mit Prädikat – is a quality wine that has no added sugar. Quality wines can be:

Kabinett – (the grapes are picked early and the wine is drier);

Spätlese – (the grapes are picked late and are probably sweeter);

Auslese, **Beerenauslese** and **Trockenbeerenauslese** – (sweeter wines).

Zum Wohl! [ts-oom vole] *Cheers!*
Prost! [proost] *Cheers!*

▶ Dialogue 6

Kellner (waiter)	Sie (you)
Was darf es sein?	
	Ich möchte ein Glas Wein, ein Glas Bier und eine Tasse Kaffee.
Rotwein oder Weißwein?	
	Weißwein.
Süß oder trocken?	
	Halbtrocken.
Bitte schön.	
	Danke.
Bitte.	
	Zahlen, bitte!
Das macht 5 (fünf) Euro.	

Learning notes

- Read both parts of the dialogue out loud.
- Cover up the right-hand side and practise ordering drinks.

Exercise 3

What would you say if you wanted to order the following?

e f g

Revision

1 Imagine Herr Braun has come to see you.
How would you ask him:
a what the journey was like?
b if he would like something to drink?
c if he would like milk and sugar in his coffee?
d if he would like a piece of cake?

2 Now you are visiting Herr und Frau Braun in Germany. Pair up the following questions and answers.

a Wie geht es Ihnen?   i Gerne.
b Trinken Sie ein Glas Wein? ii Ja, bitte.
c Rotwein oder Weißwein?   iii Weißwein.
d Süß oder trocken?   iv Gut, danke.
e Noch ein Glas? ...!   v Halbtrocken.

▶ Listening exercise 3

What have they ordered?

a The man orders a glass of i red wine ii white wine iii beer.
b The woman orders a cup of i tea ii coffee iii hot chocolate.
c The boy orders a glass of i coke ii lemonade iii milk.
d The girl orders a glass of i orange ii tomato iii apple juice.

▶ Listening exercise 4

Which is the right answer?

a The speaker says i good morning ii good day iii good evening.
b She offers you i tea ii coffee iii wine.
c She offers you i a biscuit ii a piece of lemon cake iii a piece of chocolate cake.

Sign language

1 What drinks can you get here?

Heiße Getränke

Tasse Kaffee	€2,80
Kännchen Kaffee	€5,60
Tasse Kaffee koffeinfrei	€2,80
Kännchen Kaffee koffeinfrei	€5,60
Tasse ½ Schoc + ½ Kaffee	€3,00
Kännchen ½ Schoc + ½ Kaffee	€6,00
Tasse Schokolade	€2,80
Kännchen Schokolade mit Sahne	€5,60
Kännchen Tee	€5,60
Tasse Tee mit Rum	€4,50
Glas Kamillentee	€2,80
Glas Pfefferminztee	€2,80

Imbiss	snack
Sahne	cream
Kännchen	pot

2 How would you order these for your friends?

And what would you order for yourself?

03 was kostet es?

what does it cost?

In this unit you will learn how to
- say the numbers to 100
- understand German numbers when you hear them
- use German money
- recognize German prices and telephone numbers

▶ Die Zahlen von 1 bis 20 *The numbers from 1 to 20*

0 null	5 fünf [finf]	9 neun [(an)noyn]
1 eins [(H)eins]	6 sechs [zex]	10 zehn [tsayn]
2 zwei [tsv-eye]	7 sieben [zeebun]	11 elf
3 drei [dry]	8 acht	12 zwölf [tsvulf]
4 vier [fear]		

Language notes

German numbers are easy to learn. You only have to learn the numbers 1–12 and then you can make up all the numbers to 20. For the 'teens' just add 'three', 'four' etc. to 'ten', ie.

Thirteen is 'three+ten'	**dreizehn**
Fourteen is 'four+ten'	**vierzehn**
Fifteen is 'five+ten'	**fünfzehn**
For sixteen, **sechs** loses its last '**s**':	**sechzehn**
For seventeen, **sieben** loses its '**en**':	**siebzehn**
Eighteen is 'eight+ten'	**achtzehn**
Nineteen is 'nine+ten'	**neunzehn**
Twenty is	**zwanzig**

Learning notes

- Read all the numbers out loud or listen to the recording and say the numbers after it.
- Try to say the first six numbers without looking. Now try the numbers six to 12.
- Now make up the numbers 13–20 and say them out loud. Remember that 16 and 17 need special treatment.

▶ Wo wohnen Sie? *Where do you live?*

Wie ist Ihre Adresse? [vee ist ear-uh adress-uh?]	*What is your address?*
ich wohne [ich vone-uh]	*I live*
er wohnt [air vone-t]	*he lives*
sie wohnt [see vone-t]	*she lives*
die Adresse [dee adress-uh]	*address*
die Straße [dee shtrah-suh]	*street*
die Allee [dee al-lay]	*avenue*

▶ Dialogue 7

Wo wohnen Sie?

In Berlin.

Wie ist Ihre Adresse?

Friedrichstraße 17.

Und wo wohnt Frau Zimmermann?

Sie wohnt Mozartstraße, Nummer 16.

Und Fritz Sievers?

Er wohnt Bonner Allee 9.

Und Helmut Grün?

Unter den Linden 14.

Und Boris Fischer?

Das weiß ich nicht.

Learning notes

- Practise saying both sides of the dialogue.
- Now how would you tell Herr Fischer where these people live?

Note that German addresses have the house number after rather than before the street name.

Silke Taraks	Beethovenstraße 18
Jörg Quecke	Lindenstraße 14
Sandra Müller	Bonner Allee 2
Christian Schulz	Auf dem Hang 7

Exercise 1

Put these numbers in the right order:

sechs   fünfzehn   zehn   neunzehn   fünf   siebzehn   sieben
vier   dreizehn   eins   acht   zwanzig   elf   sechzehn
zwei   vierzehn   neun   achtzehn   zwölf   drei

Exercise 2

What are these numbers? Write them out in full and say them out loud.

▶ More practice with numbers!

Wie viel? [vee feel]	*How many?*
Wie viele? [vee feel-uh]	
Wie viele Flaschen Wein?	*How many bottles of wine?*
Wie viele Tassen Tee?	*... cups of tea?*
Wie viele Eisportionen?	*... ice creams?*
Wie viel Stück Kuchen?	*How many pieces of cake?*
Was möchten Sie?	*What would you like?*
[vas murch-tun zee]	
Ich möchte ... [ich murch-tuh]	*I would like ...*

Bringen Sie mir ... [bring-en zee mere]	*Please bring me ...*
der Kellner [dare kell-nuh]	*the waiter*
Sonst noch etwas? [zonst noch etvas]	*Anything else?*
Noch was? [noch vas]	*Anything else?*
Ist das alles? [ist das al-us]	*Is that all?*

Exercise 3

a Wie viel Flaschen Wein?

d Wie viel Stück Apfelstrudel?

b Wie viel Glas Bier?

e Wie viel Stück Kuchen?

c Wie viel Eisportionen?

f Wie viele Tassen Tee?

i Apfelstrudel is a dessert made with apple, cinnamon and raisins wrapped in a thin envelope of filo or flaky pastry cooked and served with a dusting of *icing sugar* **Puderzucker**.

Ich möchte *I would like*

▶ Dialogue 8

Sie	der Kellner
	Was möchten Sie?
Ich möchte vier Gläser Wein.	
	Rotwein oder Weißwein?
Drei Gläser Weißwein und ein Glas Rotwein.	
	Noch was?
Zwei Gläser Limonade, und zwei Tassen Kaffee.	
	Noch was?
Ja. Acht Stück Apfelstrudel.	
	Ist das alles?
Ja, danke.	

Learning note

• Practise your part of the dialogue.

Exercise 4

Now see if you can ask for these:

a b c
d e f

▶ Listening exercise 5

Schreiben Sie die Nummern auf! *Listen and write down the numbers.*

▶ Die Zahlen von 20 bis 100 *The numbers from 20 to 100*

Word patterns

You have seen that German numbers 1–20 are very easy to learn. If you know the numbers to 12 and the number for 20 you can make all the other numbers. From **zwanzig** *twenty* you can see that the equivalent of the English ending *-ty* is **-zig**. To create the other 'tens', 'three', 'four', 'five' etc. are placed before **-zig**.

zwanzig	20
dreißig	30
vierzig	40
fünfzig	50
sechzig	60
siebzig	70
achtzig	80
neunzig	90
(ein)hundert	100

Note the following:

dreißig	ß instead of z
sechzig	**sech(s)zig: sechs** loses its **-s**
siebzig	**sieb(en)zig: sieben** loses its **-en**

Now look at the numbers from 21 to 29:

21	einundzwanzig
22	zweiundzwanzig
23	dreiundzwanzig
24	vierundzwanzig
25	fünfundzwanzig
26	sechsundzwanzig
27	siebenundzwanzig
28	achtundzwanzig
29	neunundzwanzig

Language notes

When you say a two-digit number such as 21 you say the unit (or right-hand digit) first: one.

To make it easier there is a dot under the digit which you have to say first in the exercises on the next page.

To complete your knowledge of German numbers, here are the words for a hundred, a thousand and a million:

100	(ein)hundert
1,000	(ein)tausend
1,000,000	eine Million

Was macht das? *How much is it?*

▶ Dialogue 9

Sie	Kellnerin
	Was möchten Sie?
Ich möchte vier Gläser Wein und vier Flaschen Bier.	
	Bitte schön.
Was macht das?	
	Das macht €32.
	Was darf es sein?
Ich möchte vier Tassen Tee und drei Tassen Kaffee.	
	Bitte schön.
Was macht das?	
	€19,60.
	Was darf es sein?
Ich möchte zwei Stück Kuchen und fünf Tassen Kaffee.	
	Bitte schön.
Was macht das?	
	€21.

Was darf es sein?	*What can I get you?*
[vas darf es zine?]	(lit: *what may it be?*)
Was kostet das?	*How much does it cost?*
Wie teuer ist das?	*How much is it?*
[vee toy-er ist das?]	

Learning notes

- Practise your parts of the dialogues.
- **Was kostet das?** Read the prices out loud.

eine Tasse Tee   eine Tasse Kaffee   ein Stück Torte

ein Glas Rotwein   ein Glas Bier   eine Flasche   ein Becher Kaffee
Mineralwasser

Here is some more practice to help you get used to the sound of the numbers.

Exercise 5

Look at these numbers and say them in German.

Say the digit with the dot under it *first*.

a 21   b 25   c 32   d 36   e 43   f 47   g 54   h 58
i 61   j 69   k 72   l 75   m 84   n 88   o 92   p 99

▶ Listening exercise 6

Now listen and write down which of the above numbers is being said. (If you haven't got the recording, try to get someone to read them to you in a different order.)

▶ Listening exercise 7

Put a ring round the word you hear. (If you haven't got the recording, practise saying both words and listen to the difference or try to get someone to read them to you.)

a	24	42	f	67	76
b	32	23	g	93	39
c	25	52	h	29	92
d	46	64	i	48	84
e	38	83	j	62	26

ℹ Germans often say their telephone numbers (apart from the code) in twos: e.g. **25 42 89** would be said as **fünfundzwanzig, zweiundvierzig, neunundachtzig.**

The dialling code is called **die Vorwahl** [dee for-vahl].

The international code for England from Germany is 00 44: **null, null, vier, vier.** You then drop the 0 before your own area code, eg. 00 44(UK) -20 (London) 7743 4163.

Now tell a German friend what number he/she needs to ring you from Germany.

Revision

Although it is easy to say the German numbers, it is not so easy to recognize them, especially when they are spoken quickly.

▶ Listening exercise 8

How much does it cost? Put a ring round the price you hear. (If you don't have the recording try to get someone to say one number from each pair in German for you.)

a	€2,50	or	€5,20	f	€4,75	or	€4,25
b	€12,80	or	€8,20	g	€14,10	or	€40,10
c	€16,50	or	€60,50	h	€45,00	or	€54,00
d	€34,60	or	€43,60	i	€25,00	or	€52,00
e	€50,00	or	€15,00	j	€72,90	or	€27,90

1 Now try to order these:

2 Read the details given about these six people. How old are they and what are their telephone numbers?

a Name: *Franz Schmidt*
   Alter: *45*
   Telefon: *31 53 27*

d Name: *Helmut Grün*
   Alter: *28*
   Telefon: *48 02 49*

b Name: *Marion Braun*
   Alter: *17*
   Telefon: *22 95 78*

e Name: *Silke Müller*
   Alter: *32*
   Telefon: *53 66 31*

c Name: *Elisabeth Ant*
   Alter: *48*
   Telefon: *87 46 03*

c Name: *Paul Schreiber*
   Alter: *67*
   Telefon: *35 64 77*

3 Can you say how much these cost?

i	white wine	€11,20	**iv**	ice	€1,63
ii	red wine	€9,30	**v**	pizza	€9,35
iii	beer	€2,10			

04

das Alphabet

the alphabet

In this unit you will learn how to
- say the alphabet
- ask someone to spell their name or where they come from
- spell your own name and address
- spell difficult words
- use the correct form of the word 'you'

Wie schreibt man das? *How do you spell it?*

▶ Das Alphabet *The alphabet*

a – *ah*   b – *bay*   c – *tsay*   d – *day*   e – *ay*   f – *eff*   g – *gay*

h – *hah*   i – *ee*   j – *yot*   k – *kah*   l – *ell*   m – *emm*   n – *enn*

o – *oh*   p – *pay*   q – *koo*   r – *air*   s – *es*   t – *tay*   u – *ooh*

v – *fow*   w – *vay*   x – *icks*   y – *ipsilon*   z – *tset*

ä – *eh*   äu – *oy*   ö – *er*   ü – *euh*   ß – *ess*

nn = doppel n

ß = s *tset or* scharfes s

Pronunciation tip

Letters to watch:

a – *ah*   v – *fow*

e – *ay*   w – *vay*

i – *ee*

Learning notes

- Practise saying the alphabet (after the recording if possible) and check your pronunciation.
- Write down the sound of the letters you need to spell your own name and learn them off by heart.
- **Wie schreibt man das?** *How do you spell it?* (lit: how does one write it?).
- Practise spelling these names out loud:
  Peter   Martin   Susanne   Ulrike   Florian

▶ Dialogue 10

Sie	Herr Meyer
Wie heißen Sie?	
	Meyer.
Wie schreibt man das?	
	M E Y E R.
Und wo wohnen Sie, Herr Meyer?	
	In Mannheim.

Mit doppel 'n'?

Ja.

Wo sind Sie geboren?

In Würzburg.

Wie schreibt man das?

W Ü R Z B U R G.

Vielen Dank.

Nichts zu danken.

Learning notes

- Practise saying both sides of the dialogue.
- Answer these questions yourself:
  Wie heißen Sie? ...
  Wie schreibt man das? ...
  Und wo wohnen Sie? ...
  Wie schreibt man das? ...
- How would you spell these places in German?
  Chipping Norton   Edinburgh   Conwy   Norfolk
  Stratford   York   Waverley   Oxford

Wie heißen Sie?/Wie heißt du? *What's your name?*

Language notes: *Sie* or *du*?

Sie – *you*

There are three words for *you* in German. The most important one to learn is the 'polite' form which you use when addressing people older than yourself and people you don't know very well.

This is the form you have been using so far:

Wie heißen Sie?	*What is your name?* (lit: How are you called?)
Wo wohnen Sie?	*Where do you live?*
Haben Sie einen Stadtplan?	*Have you got a town plan?*
Wie geht es Ihnen?	*How are you?* (lit: How goes it to you?)

Du – *you*

This form is used when talking to a child or someone you know well. You would not normally use it to an adult until they invite you to. If you know someone well they may say: **Duzen wir uns.** This means you should use **du** instead of **Sie**.

> **Wie heißt du?**   **Wo wohnst du?**   **Hast du einen Stadtplan?**
> **Wie geht es dir?** *How are you?* (lit: How goes it to you?)

If you call each other by your first names you can usually start to use the **du** form.

Ihr – *you*

The third form is the plural of **du**. You use it with a group of children or people that you know well.

(Concentrate on learning the other two forms first and come back to this later when you are more confident with the other two forms.)

Word patterns

When using the **Sie** form the verb ends with **-en**.
When using the **du** form the verb ends with **-st**.

> **Kommen Sie mit dem Auto?**   **Spielen Sie Tennis?**
> **Kommst du mit dem Auto?**   **Spielst du Tennis?**
> *Are you coming by car?*   *Do you play tennis?*

Exercise 1

Sie form or **du** form? Find the right form.
You are talking to Frau Schneider. How would you ask her:

a How are you?
b When are you coming to London?
c What are you doing tomorrow?
d Do you like playing tennis?
e Do you like swimming?
f Would you like a cup of coffee?

Exercise 2

Now you are talking to Frau Schneider's 13-year-old daughter Melanie. Ask her the same questions, choosing the right ones from those listed below:

a Wie geht es dir?
b Was machst du morgen?
c Wann kommen Sie nach London?
d Schwimmen Sie gern?
e Spielst du gern Tennis?
f Wie geht es dir?
g Was machst du morgen?
h Trinkst du gern eine Tasse Kaffee?
i Trinken Sie gern eine Tasse Kaffee?
j Wie geht es Ihnen?
k Was machen Sie morgen?
l Wann kommst du nach London?
m Schwimmst du gern?
n Spielen Sie gern Tennis?
o Was machen Sie morgen?

Exercise 3

Meet Herr Meyer's 12-year-old daughter. Ask her her name.

b Which form are you going to use?
b Ask her how she is.
c Now ask her if she would like a cup of coffee or a glass of orange juice.

▶ Listening exercise 9

Which form is being used in each of the sentences you hear?

▶ An der Rezeption *At reception*

Wie schreibt man das?	*How do you write it?*
Wie buchstabiert man das?	*How do you spell it?*
Langsamer, bitte.	*Slower, please.*
[lang-zah-muh]	

der Name [dare nah-muh]	name
die Postleitzahl [dee post-lite-tsahl]	postcode
die Vorwahl [dee for-vahl]	dialling code
der Vorname [dare for-nah-muh]	first name
der Nachname/Familienname [dare nach-nah-muh/familien-nah-muh]	surname
der Bindestrich	hyphen
der Buchstabe	letter (character)

▶ Dialogue 11

Listen to (or read) these short conversations:

Wie heißen Sie?

König.

Wie schreibt man das?

K Ö N I G.

Und mit Vornamen?

Elke.

Wie buchstabiert man das?

E L K E.

Wie heißt du?

Susanne.

Wie schreibt man das?

S U S A N N E.

Und wie lautet dein Nachname?

Hoffmann.

Mit doppel f?

Ja, und doppel n.

Wie heißen Sie?

Fischer.

Wie schreibt man das?

F I S C H E R.

Und mit Vornamen?

Hans-Peter.

Mit Bindestrich?

Ja.

Wie heißen Sie?

Mein Name ist
Kistenmacher.

Wie schreibt man das?

KISTENMACHER.

Langsamer bitte!

KISTENMACHER.

Learning note

* Practise reading both parts of the dialogues.

▶ Listening exercise 10

Wie heißen Sie? *What's your name?*

Write the names of the six people.

▶ Dialogue 12

Empfangsdame	Herr Nabockwicz
Wie heißen Sie?	
	Jürgen Nabockwicz.
Wie schreibt man das?	
	NABOCKWICZ.
Wie bitte?	
	NABOCKWICZ.
Woher kommen Sie?	
	Aus Lodz.
Wie schreibt man das?	
	LODZ.
Langsamer, bitte!	
	LODZ.
Staatsangehörigkeit?	
	Polnisch.
Wie ist Ihre Adresse hier in Deutschland?	
	Eichhornweg 63, Dortmund-Applerbeck.

Schreibt man das mit
Bindestrich?

Ja.

Und doppel p?

Ja.

Wie ist die Postleitzahl?

44267.

Und die Telefonnummer?

01 23 45.

Und die Vorwahl für
Dortmund?

0230.

Unterschreiben Sie hier.
Vielen Dank, auf
Wiedersehen.

Learning notes

- Practise both sides of the conversation.
- Now give your own answers to the receptionist's questions.

▶ Listening exercise 11

Where do these 12 people live? Write down the details they give.

Revision

1   Welcher Buchstabe fehlt? *Which letter is missing?*

   a Toi.ette
   b Ca.é
   c B.r
   d Restau.ant

   e Ho.el
   f Ba.nhof
   g Stadtzentru.
   h Flu.hafen

2   A little boy is playing with John at the campsite.

   a Ask him his name.
   b Ask where he is from.
   c Would he like a drink of lemonade?

   John would like you to ask the little boy to play tennis with
   him.

   d What are you going to ask?

3 **Sie** or **du**? Add the correct ending

a Was mach.. du morgen?
b Was mach.. Sie morgen?
c Wann komm.. Sie nach London?
d Wann komm.. du nach London?
e Schwimm.. Sie gern?
f Schwimm.. du gern?
g Spiel.. du gern Tennis?
h Spiel.. Sie gern Tennis?
i Was mach.. du morgen?
j Was mach.. Sie morgen?
k Trink.. du gern eine Tasse Kaffee?
l Trink.. Sie gern eine Tasse Kaffee?

Sign language

Read the letters on these signs (look back at the alphabet on page 33 to check the pronunciation of the letters).

USA

Pkw

GmbH

DB

WDR

AG

EU   BRD

Now see if you can match them up with their meanings.

Volkswagen German car manufacturer
Deutsche Bahn German railways
Bayerische Motorenwerke German car manufacturer
Deutsche Mark former German currency
Europäische Union European Union
Bundesrepublik Deutschland Federal Republic of Germany
Gesellschaft mit beschränkter Haftung limited company (ltd)
Personenkraftwagen car!
die Vereinigten Staaten the United States
Aktiengesellschaft public limited company (Plc)
Westdeutscher Rundfunk German radio and TV company

Quiz

1 What would you do with a *Wiener Schnitzel*?
 a Wear it **b** Dance it **c** Eat it
2 Who is your *Oma*?
 a Your mother **b** Your grandmother **c** Your washing powder
3 Where would you find the *Kölner Dom*?
 a In Munich **b** In Koblenz **c** in Cologne
4 What would you do with a *Schwarzwälder Kirschtorte*?
 a Not know how to spell it **b** Not know how to say it **c** Eat it
5 Your friend invites you to go to a *Kneipe*. **a** You say yes **b** You ask what time the show begins **c** You ask if you should take your swimming costume
6 *Lufthansa* is: **a** The German national anthem **b** The German national airline **c** The highest mountain in Germany
7 You are going to a party and are asked to bring a *Lederhose*. You would: **a** Wear it **b** Eat it **c** Drink it
8 What is the English for these towns? **a** München **b** Köln **c** Stuttgart **d** Wien
9 Which of these are rivers and what are they called in English? **a** Der Rhein **b** Die Mosel **c** Die Donau **d** Die Zugspitze
10 At a party you are offered *Glühwein*. What should you do with it? **a** Drink it **b** Smoke it **c** Pour it into the nearest plant pot
11 Tie breaker for the real expert!
 There are 16 *Bundesländer* in Germany. Can you pair up the *Bundesländer* with their capitals?

Baden-Württemberg	Saarbrücken
Bayern	Hannover
Berlin	Potsdam
Brandenburg	München
Bremen	Mainz
Hamburg	Wiesbaden
Hessen	Bremen
Mecklenburg-Vorpommern	Schwerin
Niedersachsen	Stuttgart
Nordrhein-Westfalen	Hamburg
Rheinland-Pfalz	Berlin
Saarland	Dresden
Sachsen	Magdeburg
Sachsen-Anhalt	Kiel
Schleswig-Holstein	Erfurt
Thüringen	Düsseldorf

05 an der Rezeption
at reception

In this unit you will learn how to
- give your particulars when booking into a hotel
- ask for and give an address and postcode
- ask for and give a telephone number
- ask for the telephone code
- say where you come from and what nationality you are
- fill in a form

▶ Im Hotel *In the hotel*

der Name [dare nah-muh]	*name*
die Adresse [dee add-ress-uh]	*address*
die Postleitzahl	postcode
[dee post-lite-tsahl]	
die Handynummer	*mobile number*
[dee handy-numm-uh]	
die Telefonnummer	*telephone number*
[dee tele-fone-numm-uh]	
die Vorwahl [dee for-vahl]	*dialling code*
das Zimmer [das tsim-mer]	*room*
wählen [vair-lun]	*to dial* (lit: to choose)
besetzt [buh-zetst]	*engaged*
frei [fry]	*free, vacant*
Wie ist …? [vee ist]	*What is …?* (lit: how is …?)
Sind Sie …? [zint zee]	*Are you …?*
Wie ist Ihre Adresse?	*What* (lit: how) *is your address?*
und Ihre Telefonnummer?	*and your phone number?*
Haben Sie ein Zimmer frei?	*Have you a room free?*
die Empfangsdame	*the receptionist*

Learning notes

- Practise saying the new words and phrases out loud.
- Cover up the English and see if you can remember what they all mean.
- Now cover up the German and see if you can remember what it should be.

▶ Dialogue 13

Herr Braun	**die Empfangsdame**
Haben Sie ein Zimmer frei?	
	Ja. Wie heißen Sie?
Braun.	
	Und mit Vornamen, Herr Braun?
Wilfrid.	
	Und Ihre Adresse?
Dortmunder Straße 53, Stuttgart.	
	Und die Postleitzahl?
70376.	
	Wie bitte?
70376.	

53 14 25 74.

Darf ich Ihre Telefonnummer haben?

Wie ist die Vorwahl für Stuttgart?

0711.

0170 85 76 32 48 90.

Und die Handynummer?

Und haben Sie eine E-Mail-Adresse?

Ja: WilfridB123@web.de

Also, Zimmer 46.
Hier ist der Schlüssel.

Vielen Dank.

Bitte schön.

Pronunciation tips

v sounds f and w sounds v
ie sounds ee and ei sounds aye
z sounds ts
ß is ss

Learning notes

- Read the dialogue out loud and check you understand it. Take care with the pronunciation.
- Cover up the dialogue and listen to the recording. Can you understand all the numbers?
- Now cover up the left-hand side and give your own answers to the questions!

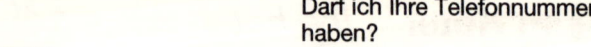 Woher kommen Sie? *Where are you from?*

Woher kommen Sie? [vo-hair common zee?]	*Where are you from?*
Ich bin ... [ich bin]	*I am ...*
Ich komme aus ... [ich comme-uh (h)ouse]	*I come from ...*
England [ehnglant]	*England*
Engländer [ehng-lenn-duh]	*Englishman*
Engländerin [ehng-lendur-in]	*Englishwoman*
Deutschland [doy-tsch-lant]	*Germany*
Österreich [ur-stir-righ(t)-ch]	*Austria*

Word patterns

In German you sometimes use different forms of a word according to whether it is a man or woman who is speaking.

For instance to say *I am English*, a man would say **Ich bin Engländer**, but a woman would say **Ich bin Engländerin**.

The feminine version of the words is usually made by adding -**in** to the masculine form. For example:

Ich bin Brite/Britin.	Ich komme aus Großbritannien.
Ich bin Engländer/-in.	Ich komme aus England.
Ich bin Schotte/Schottin.	Ich komme aus Schottland.
Ich bin Waliser/-in.	Ich komme aus Wales.
Ich bin Ire/Irin.	Ich komme aus Irland.
Ich bin Australier/-in.	Ich komme aus Australien.
Ich bin Neuseeländer/-in.	Ich komme aus Neuseeland.
Ich bin Schweizer/-in.	Ich komme aus der Schweiz.
Ich bin Amerikaner/-in.	Ich komme aus Amerika *or* aus den Vereinigten Staaten.

die Vereinigten Staaten *the United States*
die Schweiz *Switzerland*

Neighbours to Germany may say:

Ich bin Pole/Polin.
Ich bin Belgier/-in.
Ich bin Österreicher/-in.
Ich bin Holländer/-in.
Ich bin Franzose/Französin.
Ich bin Italiener/-in.

Pronunciation tips

au sounds **ow** as in **ow**(l)
ch is pronounced as in the Scottish word lo**ch**
i in Brite and Amerikaner is short, as in *it*, but is long in Ire, as in *deep*

Europa *Europe*

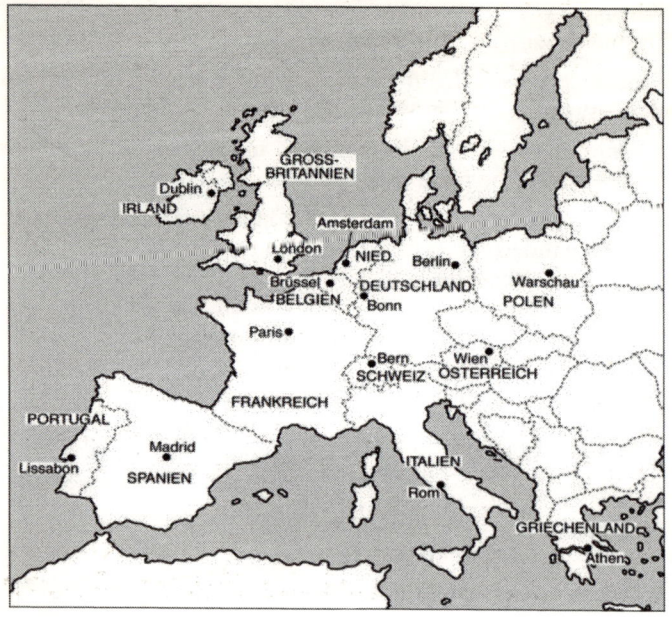

Exercise 1

What is the German for?

a Germany _____

b France _____

c Italy _____

d Poland _____

e Ireland _____

f Great Britain _____

g Belgium _____

h Spain _____

i Austria _____

j England _____

k Scotland _____

l Holland _____

m Portugal _____

n Switzerland _____

o Wales _____

▶ Listening exercise 12

Welche Staatsangehörigkeit haben sie und woher kommen sie? *What nationality are they and where are they from?* Listen to the ten people talking about themselves and write down what they say.

Word building

Look in the list and work out what **Geburts-** means. You already know the word for *day* as in *Good day*! Now join the two words to form the word *birthday*: **Geburtstag**.

What does the word **Ort** mean? (look at **Geburtsort** and **Wohnort**).

> # Ortsende

You often see this sign when leaving a small town or village. It means you are leaving the 'place' and there will usually be a speed derestriction sign beside it.

Bade- means bath or bathing; combining it with **Ort** gives us the German word for a *spa town* or *bathing resort*: **Badeort** [bah-duh-ort].

▶ Ein Formular zum Ausfüllen *A form to fill in*

Vorname [for-nahmuh]	*first name*
Familienname [familien-nahmuh]	*surname* (lit: family name)
Wohnort [vone-ort]	*home/domicile*
Anschrift [an-shrift]	*address*
Staatsangehörigkeit [shtahts-an-guh-her-ich-kite]	*nationality*
Geburtsort [geboorts-ort]	*birthplace*
Geburtsdatum [geboorts-daht-um]	*date of birth*
Familienstand [familien-shtant]	*family status*
verheiratet [fair-high-ratet]	*married*
ledig [lay-dich]	*unmarried*
Ihren Ausweis [ear-en ows-vice]	*your identity card*
Ihr Pass [ear pass]	*your passport*
Ihre Kreditkarte [ear-uh credit cart-uh]	*your credit card*

Pronunciation tips

ow as in **owl**
v sounds **f**
w sounds **v**

Learning notes

- Practise saying the new words out loud.
- Cover up the English and see if you can remember what they all mean. Look for ways of remembering new words.

Name: *Fischer*   Vorname: *Helmut*

Geburtsdatum: *22.07.65*

Anschrift: *Waldstraße 34, Stuttgart*

Postleitzahl: *70597*   Telefonnummer: *12 34 56*

Staatsangehörigkeit: *Österreicher*

Geburtsort: *Salzburg*   Familienstand: *ledig*

Ausweis/Reisepass: *137239815*

Unterschrift: *H. Fischer*   Datum: *2004.04.03*
(signature)

Exercise 2

What do you know about Herr Fischer? Answer the questions below:

a What is his first name?
b What is his address?
c What nationality is he?
d Is he married or single?

e How old is he?
f What is his phone number?
g Where was he born?
h What is his postcode?

▶ Listening exercise 13

Listen and see if you can fill in this form.

Name:	Vorname:
Wohnort:	
Postleitzahl:	Telefonnummer:
Staatsangehörigkeit:	Familienstand:
Geburtsort:	Geburtsdatum:
Ausweis/Reisepass:	

Exercise 3

Jetzt sind Sie dran! *Now it's your turn.*

You are at the Hotel Stern (star) in Frankfurt. Practise your part of the dialogue.

a *Ask if they have a room free.*

Empfangsdame Ja. Wie heißen Sie?
Und mit Vornamen?

b ....

Empfangsdame Woher kommen Sie?

c ....

Empfangsdame Staatsangehörigkeit?

d ....

Empfangsdame Und Ihre Adresse?

e ....

Empfangsdame Und die Postleitzahl?

f ....

Empfangsdame Wie bitte?

g ....

Empfangsdame Und Ihre Telefonnummer?

h ....

Empfangsdame Wie ist die Vorwahl?

i ....

Empfangsdame Und Ihre Mobile-Nummer?

j ....

Empfangsdame Haben Sie eine E-Mail-Adresse?

k ....

Empfangsdame Also, Zimmer 15.
Hier ist der Schlüssel.

l ....

Empfangsdame Bitte schön.

Exercise 3

Wie hießen die Fragen? *What were the questions that produced these replies?*

a ....? Schneider.
b ....? Hans.
c ....? Deutsch.
d ....? Dortmund. Am Hang 35.
e ....? 44267
f ....? 23 54 63
g ....? 23 54 63
h ....? 0230

Revision

Ein Formular zum Ausfüllen *A form to fill in*

Now fill in this form with your own details:

Name:	Vorname:
Anschrift:	
Postleitzahl:	Telefonnummer:
Staatsangehörigkeit:	Familienstand:
Geburtsort:	Geburtsdatum:
Ausweis/Reisepass:	
Unterschrift: (signature)	Datum:

06

im Hotel

in the hotel

In this unit you will learn how to
- book in to a hotel
- ask where things are
- ask when things are
- ask to pay the bill
- say if anything is wrong
- understand how to use the phone

▶ An der Rezeption *At reception*

Haben Sie ...?	*Have you ...?*
ein/das Zimmer	*a/the room*
Einzelzimmer	*single room*
Doppelzimmer	*double room*
Wie lange?	*How long (for)?*
die Nacht (die Nächte)	*night (nights)*
das Bad	*bath*
die Dusche	*shower*
das Telefon	*telephone*
Wie viel kostet es?	*How much does it cost?*
das Frühstück	*breakfast*
Ist das Frühstück inbegriffen?	*Is breakfast included?*
Um wie viel Uhr ...?	*At what time?*
ab ... bis	*from ... to*
im dritten Stock	*on the third floor*
der Fahrstuhl	*lift*
dort drüben	*over there*
bleiben	*to stay or remain*
Würden Sie sich bitte eintragen?	*Would you sign in, please?*

Learning notes

- Read the German words out loud. How many can you remember?
- Decide which it would be useful to learn and which you will only need to recognize. Look for ways to remember the useful phrases.
- Cover them up and see how many you can remember.

Exercise 1

How are you going to ask: *Have you a ...?*

a single room with shower
b double room with bath
c single room with bath
d double room with shower

Exercise 2

Can you remember the word for *where*?

How would you ask:

a Where is the room?
b Where is the lift?
c Where is the telephone?

▶ Dialogue 14

Sie	Empfangsdame
Haben Sie ein Zimmer frei?	
	Einzelzimmer oder Doppelzimmer?
Doppelzimmer.	
	Ja. Wie lange bleiben Sie?
Zwei Nächte.	
	Mit Bad oder mit Dusche?
Mit Bad. Wie viel kostet es?	
	€70.
Und was kostet ein Zimmer mit Dusche?	
	€65.
Ist das Frühstück inbegriffen?	
	Ja.
Ich nehme das Zimmer mit Dusche. Um wie viel Uhr ist das Frühstück?	
	Ab 6.00 Uhr.
Bis wann?	
	Bis 9.00 Uhr. Zimmer 307 im dritten Stock. Der Fahrstuhl ist dort drüben. Würden Sie sich bitte eintragen? Hier ist der Schlüssel.

Learning notes

- Make sure you understand all the dialogue.
- Read both parts of the dialogue out loud.
- Cover up the left-hand part and work out what to say.

▶ **Listening exercise 14**

Listen to the six customers making their reservations. What sort of rooms do they want? How long are they staying?

Ich möchte ... *I would like ...*

What other things might you want to ask or say?
Here are some suggestions.

Haben Sie ...	*Have you ...*
Haben Sie ein Familienzimmer?	*Have you a family room?*
Haben Sie ein Zimmer ...?	*Have you got a room ...?*
... mit Doppelbett	*with a double bed*
... mit Einzelbetten	*with single beds*
... mit Zusatzbett	*with an extra bed*
Haben Sie etwas Billigeres?	*Have you anything cheaper?*
Haben Sie eine Garage?	*Have you a garage?*
Haben Sie ein Zimmer mit Balkon?	*Have you a room with a balcony?*
Haben Sie ein Zimmer mit Fernseher?	*Have you a room with television?*
Haben Sie ein Zimmer mit Telefon?	*Have you a room with a phone?*
Ich möchte ...	*I would like to ...*
Ich möchte nach England anrufen	*I would like to ring England*
Ich möchte im Zimmer frühstücken	*I would like to have breakfast in my room*
Ich möchte das Fenster öffnen	*I would like to open the window*
Ich möchte die Heizung ausmachen	*I would like to turn off the heating*
Ich möchte zahlen	*I would like to pay*
Ich möchte eine Quittung	*I would like to a receipt*
Gibt es ...	*Is there ...*
Gibt es eine Garage?	*Is there a garage?*
Gibt es eine Tiefgarage?	*Is there a an underground garage?*

Gibt es einen Parkplatz?	*Is there a car park?*
Gibt es ein Schwimmbad?	*Is there a swimming pool?*
Gibt es einen Fitnessraum?	*Is there a fitness room?*
Gibt es eine Bar?	*Is there a bar?*
Gibt es ein Restaurant?	*Is there a restaurant?*
Gibt es ein Telefon im Zimmer?	*Is there a telephone in the room?*
Ich habe ein Zimmer reserviert.	*I have booked (reserved) a room. (lit. I have a room booked.)*
Würden Sie mich um ... wecken?	*Would you wake me at ...?*
Nehmen Sie (Kredit) Karten?	*Do you take (credit) cards?*
Unterschreiben Sie hier.	*Sign here.*

Note that with **der** words **ein** becomes **einen** after **ich möchte ...**, **haben Sie ...?**, **gibt es ...** and many other verbs, e.g.:

Gibt es einen Fitnessraum im Hotel?

(See Unit 8 for more information about **der, die** and **das**.)

Learning notes

- Practise reading all the phrases out loud.
- If possible find someone to read out phrases to you at random and see if you can recognize the meaning.
- Learn the three key phrases:
  Haben Sie ...?
  Ich möchte ...
  Gibt es ...?
- Cover up the German and see how many of the phrases you can remember.

Exercise 3

Now you should be ready to complete your part of these dialogues.

a **You**	I have booked a room.
Empfangschef	Ihr Name bitte?

b **You**	Give your name.
Empfangschef	Doppelzimmer mit Bad?

c **You**	No. Single with shower.
Empfangschef	Ach, ja. Zimmernummer 35.

d **You**	Pardon?
Empfangschef	35. Im dritten Stock.

e	**You**	Is there a lift?
	Empfangschef	Ja, dort drüben.
f	**You**	When is breakfast?
	Empfangschef	Ab 6.00 Uhr.
g	**You**	Can I have a call at 7 o'clock?
	Empfangschef	Ja. Hier ist Ihr Schlüssel.
h	**You**	Have you got a room free?
	Empfangschef	Ja. Für wie lange?
i	**You**	For three nights
	Empfangschef	Einzelzimmer oder Doppelzimmer?
j	**You**	Double.
	Empfangschef	Mit Bad oder Dusche?
k	**You**	Bath. Is there a telephone in the room?
	Empfangschef	Ja. Und Fernseher.
l	**You**	How much does it cost?
	Empfangschef	€73 pro Nacht.
m	**You**	Is breakfast included?
	Empfangschef	Ja.
n	**You**	Say you would like your bill.
	Empfangschef	Zimmernummer?
o	**You**	811. Do you take credit cards?
	Empfangschef	Ja. Unterschreiben Sie hier, bitte.
p	**You**	A receipt please.
	Empfangschef	Bitte schön.
q	**You**	Ask if you can be woken.
	Empfangschef	Ja, um wie viel Uhr?
r	**You**	At 7 o'clock.
	Empfangschef	Welche Zimmernummer haben Sie?
s	**You**	207.

Was ist los? *What's wrong?*

... funktioniert nicht	*... doesn't work*
die Heizung	*heating*
das Fenster	*window*
der Wasserhahn	*water tap*
das Licht	*light*

der Föhn	*hairdryer*
der Safe	*safe*
die Dusche	*shower*
der Schalter	*switch*
Das Zimmer ist ...	*The room is ...*
Das Zimmer ist zu laut	*The room is too noisy*
Das Zimmer ist zu klein	*The room is too small*
Das Zimmer ist zu kalt	*The room is too cold*
Das Zimmer ist zu heiß	*The room is too hot*
Das Zimmer ist zu teuer	*The room is too expensive*
Es gibt (kein/keine/keinen ...)	*There's no ...*
Es gibt kein Telefon	*There's no telephone*
Es gibt kein Bad	*There's no bath*
Es gibt keine Bar	*There's no bar*
Es gibt keinen Fernseher	*There's no TV*
Die Heizung funktioniert nicht.	*The heating doesn't work.*
Das Licht ist kaputt.	*The light is broken.*
Jemand kommt gleich.	*Someone will be right with you.*
Welche Zimmernummer haben Sie?	*What is your room number?*
Wie funktioniert ...?	*How does ... work?*
Ich nehme es.	*I'll take it.*
der Zimmerservice	*room service*
Ich habe meinen Schlüssel verloren.	*I have lost my key.*

Learning notes

- Learn the four key phrases:
  ... funktioniert nicht.
  Das Zimmer ist zu ...
  Es gibt kein/keine/keinen ...
  Wie funktioniert ...?

Bitte das
Zimmer aufräumen

Please make up
the room

Prière de faire
la chambre de suite

Bitte nicht stören!

Please don't
disturb!

Prière de ne pas
déranger!

Exercise 4

Now try these dialogues.

a	**You**	Excuse me, please.
	Empfangsdame	Bitte?
b	**You**	My room is too noisy.
	Empfangsdame	Das tut mir Leid. Zimmer 14 ist frei aber es hat kein Bad.
c	**You**	Is there a shower?
	Empfangsdame	Ja.
d	**You**	I'll take it.
	Empfangsdame	Hier ist der Schlüssel. Im ersten Stock, links.
e	**You**	Excuse me please.
	Empfangsdame	Bitte?
f	**You**	My room is too hot. How does the heating work?
	Empfangsdame	Es gibt einen Schalter unter dem Fenster.

Am Telefon

g	**You**	Room service?
	Empfangsdame	Ja.
h	**You**	The light is broken.
	Empfangsdame	Jemand kommt gleich. Welche Zimmernummer haben Sie?
i	**You**	48.
j	**You**	Room service?
	Empfangsdame	Ja.
k	**You**	Can you wake me at 6.00?
	Empfangsdame	Welche Zimmernummer haben Sie?
l	**You**	63. I would like breakfast in my room.
	Empfangsdame	Um wie viel Uhr?
m	**You**	7am.

▶ Ich möchte nach England telefonieren
I want to ring England

Wie ist die Nummer für die Telefonauskunft?	*What is the number for directory inquiries?*
Sie wählen ...	*You dial ...*
11834 für Ausland	*11834 for abroad*
11833 für Inland	*11833 for inland*
Polizei 110	*Police 110*
Feuerwehr 112	*Fire brigade 112*
Notarzt / Rettungswagen 112	*Emergency services / ambulance 112*
Ich suche eine Nummer in Frankfurt.	*I'm looking for a number in Frankfurt.*
die Vorwahl	*code*
das Ausland	*abroad*
das Inland	*inland*
zuerst	*first*
und dann	*and then*
das Ortsgespräch	*local call*
das Ferngespräch	*long distance call*
anrufen	*to call*
drücken	*to press*
Wiederholen Sie bitte	*Please repeat*
Ich möchte bitte Herrn .../ Frau ... sprechen.	*I'd like to speak to Mr.../Mrs... please.*
Er/Sie ist nicht da.	*He/she isn't here.*
die schwarze Taste	*black key*

Word patterns: word order

When you say *I want to do something* and use **Ich möchte** the other verb goes to the end of the sentence.

Ich möchte nach Amerika **anrufen**.
Ich möchte nach Frankreich **fahren**.
Ich möchte Tennis mit Hilda **spielen**.

Exercise 5

Complete the dialogue:

a *Say you want to ring England.*

Sie wählen zuerst 0 und dann
die Vorwahl für England: 00 44.

b *Now say you want to ring
room Number 25.*

Sie wählen die Nummer 25.

c *Ring reception and ask how
to make a local call.*

Sie drücken die schwarze Taste
und wählen die Nummer.

Tell your German friend how to ring Germany from your
home.

(The code for Germany is 00 49.)

Please inform the reception if you are expecting a call and
won't be in your room.

Revision

How would you say the following in German?

1   There's no
    a telephone
    b bar
    c TV   in my room

2   My room is
    a too small
    b too hot
    c too noisy
    d too cold

3   Ask for the following in German:
    a a double room
    b a single room with shower
    c a family room
    d a room with twin bed

07

die Uhrzeiten
telling the time

In this unit you will learn how to
- tell the time in German
- ask what time it is
- recognize the days of the week in German
- make arrangements to meet

▶ Es ist …

ein Uhr	acht Uhr	fünf nach eins

Es ist …

zehn nach zwei	Viertel nach zwei	Viertel nach acht

Es ist …

Viertel vor zwei	fünf vor zwei	zehn nach drei

Es tut mir Leid.	*I am sorry.*
Ich weiß es nicht.	*I don't know (it).*

Language notes

It is easy to remember the word for quarter – **Viertel** – as it is based on **vier** *four*.

In times, **nach** means *past* and **vor** means *to* (lit: before).

The word for o'clock is **Uhr** (lit: clock).

Learning notes

- Read the times out loud.
- Cover up the words and see if you can say the times.
- Listen to the recording and check your pronunciation.

 **Dialogue 15**

Sie	Passant
Entschuldigen Sie, bitte. Wie spät ist es?	
	Es ist vier Uhr.
Danke. Entschuldigen Sie, bitte. Wie viel Uhr ist es?	
	Es ist Viertel nach vier.
Danke. Entschuldigen Sie, bitte. Wie spät ist es?	
	Es ist Viertel vor fünf.
Danke.	

Entschuldigen Sie, bitte.	*Excuse me please.*
Wie viel Uhr ist es?	*What time is it?* (lit: *how many o'clock is it?*)
Wie spät ist es?	*What time is it?* (lit: *how late is it?*)
Viertel	*quarter*
es ist ...	*it is ...*
nach	*after/past*
vor	*before/to*
die Uhr [dee Oo-er]	*clock*
die Armbanduhr	*(wrist) watch*
Geht die Uhr genau?	*Is the clock/watch right?*
Meine Uhr geht nicht.	*My watch has stopped.* (lit: *is not going.*)
Sie ist kaputto.	*It (she) is broken.*

Language notes

There are two ways to ask what time it is.
Wie spät ist es? and **Wie viel Uhr ist es?**
The answer is: **Es ist ...**

Learning note

• Read both parts of the dialogue out loud.

Exercise 1

What would you say for these times?

Es ist …

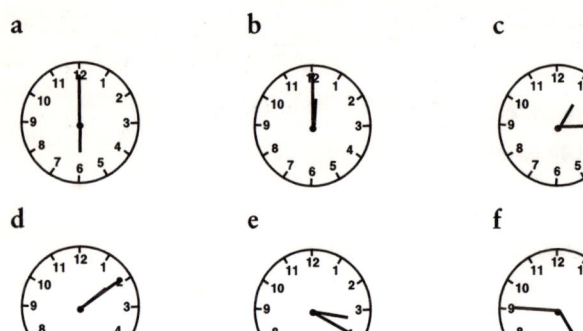

a   b   c

d   e   f

Language notes

Look at these clocks and the words. Which is the word for *half*? How can you remember it?

Halb zwei *half past one*

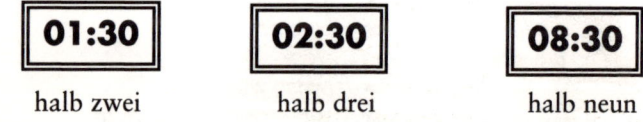

halb zwei   halb drei   halb neun

Now have another look at the words under the clock showing 1.30. Are they what you would expect them to be? What is the difference? What have you discovered about the way the Germans say half past the hour?

For 2.30, instead of saying half (*past*) two they say:

half (*to*) three.

Exercise 2

What would you say for these times? **Es ist ...**

a   b   c   d

▶ Listening exercise 15

What time is it?

a   b   c   d

Exercise 3

Jetzt sind Sie dran.

a You	Ask this gentleman the time.
Passerby	Es tut mir Leid. Ich weiß es nicht. Meine Uhr ist kaputt.

Bad luck. Try this lady.

b You	What time is it, please?
Passerby	Viertel nach elf.
c You	Thank her.
Passerby	Nichts zu danken.
d You	Say goodbye.
Passerby	Auf Wiedersehen.

Now it is your turn to be asked.

Herr X	Entschuldigung! Wie spät ist es?
e You	Oh dear, you have left your watch in the bathroom. Say you are sorry you don't know.

Exercise 4

What would you have said if it had been these times?

8.30   8.45   10.15   14.45   18.30

▶ Wann treffen wir uns? *When shall we meet?*

die Wochentage	*days of the week*
die Woche	*week*
am ...	*on ...*
am Montag	*on Monday*
am Dienstag	*on Tuesday*
am Mittwoch	*on Wednesday*
am Donnerstag	*on Thursday*
am Freitag	*on Friday*
am Samstag oder Sonnabend	*on Saturday*
am Sonntag	*on Sunday*

i There are two German words for Saturday. **Sonnabend** (lit: sun eve) is often used instead of **Samstag** in the North of Germany.

When making arrangements to meet or giving bus or train times Germans usually use the twenty-four hour clock, e.g. 5.00pm becomes 17.00 Uhr etc.

Wann treffen wir uns?	*When shall we meet? (lit: when meet we us?)*
der Morgen	*morning*
der Nachmittag	*afternoon*
der Abend	*evening*
die Nacht	*night*
Mittag	*midday*
Mitternacht	*midnight*
um	*at*
um acht Uhr morgens	*at 8 o'clock in the morning*
um acht Uhr früh	*at 8am (lit: at 8 o'clock early)*
um zwei Uhr nachmittags	*at two in the afternoon*
um sieben Uhr abends	*at seven in the evening*
Geht das?	*Is that all right? (lit: goes that?)*
Ich freue mich schon darauf.	*I am looking forward to it already.*
Bis dann!	*Till then!*

Pronunciation tips

ie sounds ee
ei sounds aye
ch as in loch
freue sounds froy-uh

Learning note

• Practise saying the days of the week.

Exercise 5

a Put these days in the right order, starting with Monday:
Samstag Donnerstag Montag Sonntag
Mittwoch Dienstag Freitag

b Put these times in the right order:

2.00h nachmittags	Mittag	9.00h früh
6.00h abends	4.00h nachmittags	19.00h
6.00h morgens	Mitternacht	

▶ Dialogue 16

Mr Taylor is staying at the Hotel Zur Post in Hamburg and rings Herr Braun to invite him out for a meal.

Mr Taylor	Herr Braun
	Braun.
Hallo, Herr Braun. Hier Mr Taylor. Ich bin im Hotel Zur Post. Essen Sie heute Abend mit uns?	
	Ja, gerne. Um wie viel Uhr?
Um acht, geht das?	
	Ja. Wann treffen wir uns?
Um halb acht in der Bar im Hotel.	
	Gut. Ich freue mich schon darauf.
Bis dann. *Auf Wiederhören!	
	Auf Wiederhören!

*Auf Wiederhören! Germans say **auf Wiederhören** (lit: *till I hear you again*), instead of **auf Wiedersehen** (lit: *till I see you again*), when using the phone.

Learning note

• Practise both parts of the dialogue.

Exercise 6

What would you say to arrange to meet at these times?

a Monday 2.30   d Tuesday 10.20   g Friday 8.45
b Thursday 23.00   e Sunday 17.45   h Tuesday midday
c Saturday 19.00   f Wednesday 17.30   i Thursday 18.15

Exercise 7

Making a phone call. How do you say:

a Goodbye.   c Till then!
b Is that all right?   d I am looking forward to it
                          already.

Revision

1 Wie viel Uhr ist es? Es ist …

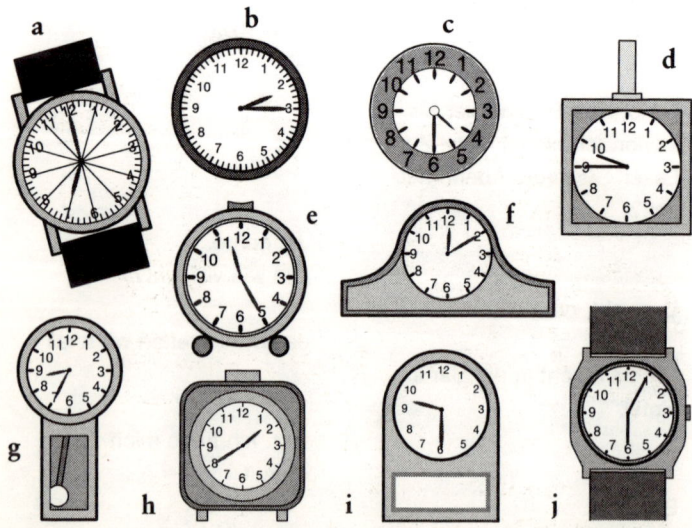

2 Und wann treffen wir uns? Wir treffen uns um …

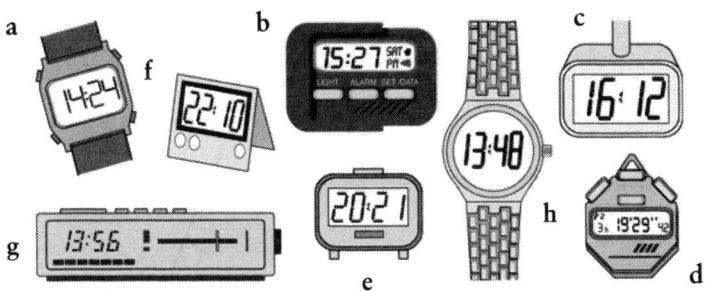

3 **Wie spät ist es?** *What's the time?* Some of these are unusual. You don't have to be able to say them all, but you should be able to work out what they mean.

a Zwanzig nach vier   **f** Fünf nach halb sieben
b Zehn nach zwei   **g** Viertel vor neun
c Halb zehn   **h** Halb drei
d Fünf nach halb elf   **i** Drei viertel vier
e Fünf vor halb vier   **j** Zehn vor neun

4 What times do the various timepieces show – and which is which in German?

a die Kuckucksuhr   **c** die Armbanduhr **e** der Wecker
b der Radiowecker   **d** die (Wand) Uhr

5 **Anagrams. Welcher Tag?** *Which day* is represented by each of these anagrams?

a STAGDINE   d MAGASST   g SNNOGDATER
b GATEFIR   e TITCHMOW
c MANGOT   f SONGANT

6 Why can't these people answer when you ask **Wie spät ist es?**

a

Ich brauche eine
Batterie für meine Uhr

b

Ich habe meine
Armbanduhr verloren

c

Meine Uhr ist kaputt

ich brauche	*I need*
verloren	*lost*

08

der Stadtplan

the street map

In this unit you will learn how to

- recognize names of important buildings in a German town
- ask where places are
- say what street they are in
- help yourself understand new words

▶ Wo ist ...? *Where is ...?*

dort drüben	*over there*
der Bahnhof	*station*
die Bibliothek	*library*
die Brücke	*bridge*
der Dom	*cathedral*
der Flughafen	*airport*
das Freibad	*open-air swimming pool*
das Informationsbüro	*information office*
die Jugendherberge	*youth hostel*
das Kino	*cinema*
die Kirche	*church*
die Kneipe	*pub*
das Krankenhaus	*hospital*
der Marktplatz	*marketplace*
das Rathaus	*town hall*
das Schloss	*castle*
der Schnellimbiss	*snack bar*
die Straße	*street*
die Hauptstraße	*main street*

And these shouldn't present much difficulty.

die Bank	**die Post**
der Park	**das Hotel**
das Restaurant	**das Theater**

Language notes

There are three German words meaning *the*: **der**, **die** and **das**. **Der** indicates a masculine word, **die** a feminine word and **das** a neuter word. Learn the **der**, **die** or **das** with each word: eg. **der Bahnhof** *the station*.

Pronunciation tips

der sounds like **dare**
die sounds like **dee**
das sounds like **das**

Learning notes

- Practise the new words.
- Check the pronunciation with the recording.
- Cover up the English and see how many you can recognize.
- Choose ten to learn today.

▶ Dialogue 17

Sie	Passant
Entschuldigen Sie bitte. Ist das die Bank?	
	Nein. Das ist das Rathaus.
Wo ist die Bank?	
	Die Bank ist dort drüben.
Danke.	
Entschuldigung! Wo ist der Bahnhof?	
	Der Bahnhof? Dort drüben!
Danke.	
Entschuldigen Sie bitte. Ist das das Hotel Zur Post?	Nein. Das ist das Hotel Modern.
Wo ist das Hotel Zur Post?	
	Es tut mir Leid. Ich weiß es nicht.
Wo ist das Informationsbüro?	
	Dort drüben.
Vielen Dank. Auf Wiedersehen.	
	Nichts zu danken. Auf Wiedersehen.

Learning note

- Read your part of the dialogue out loud.

Exercise 1

A German visitor to your town asks you:

a **Ist das die Bank?** *Tell him, no it's the post office.*
b **Wo ist die Bank?** *Tell him it's over there.*
c **Danke.** *Say: don't mention it.*
d **Wo ist das Hotel Star?** *Say you are sorry, you don't know.*
e **Wo ist das Informationsbüro?** *Tell him it's over there.*
f **Vielen Dank. Auf Wiedersehen.** *Say goodbye.*

Word patterns

Gender of nouns: *der, die* or *das* to say 'the'

This section is about the structure of the language. If all you want to do is speak and understand the language at a basic level you don't need to study it. It is better to concentrate on learning the **Key words** and useful phrases, but if you want to know more about the language and to be able to read and write it you should also try to learn something about its patterns.

A *noun* is a naming word, or a word that you can put *the* in front of in English, e.g. the table, the town centre, the hotel, the party, the pain, the shopping.

In German all nouns are either masculine, feminine or neuter, i.e. **der, die** or **das** words. **Der, die** and **das** all mean *the*. In modern English there is only one word for *the*, but in German the word for *the* changes to match the word it is going with.

Der words are masculine words : der Mann – *the man*
Die words are feminine words : die Frau – *the woman*
Das words are neuter words : das Haus – *the house*

Something else you may have noticed about nouns in German is that they all start with a capital letter.

Occasionally you can tell or guess whether the word is going to be masculine, feminine or neuter, but mostly you can't! So it's best to try to learn the **der, die** or **das** with new words or try to learn words in phrases or useful expressions, rather than as single words. You will probably find some shortcuts, however. For example, see what you notice in **Exercise 1**: What do you notice about (most) words which end with an 'e'? What about words which end with an 'o'? And foreign words (e.g. Café)?

If you want to say 'a' instead of 'the' you use **ein** or **eine**.

der words: **ein**
die words: **eine**
das words: **ein**

der Wagen *the car*   **ein Wagen** *a car*
die Katze *the cat*   **eine Katze** *a cat*
das Haus *the house*   **ein Haus** *a house*

Exercise 2

Masculine, feminine or neuter?

Bahnhof Bank Bibliothek Brücke Café Flughafen
Freibad Hotel Informationsbüro Jugendherberge Kino
Kirche Kneipe Krankenhaus Marktplatz Park Post
Rathaus Reisebüro Restaurant Schloss Schnellimbiss
Straße

der	die	das

Exercise 3

Fill in the rows, using these clues, to reveal another important
building in column A.

a a bridge   g a cinema
b a church   h an airport
c a theatre   i a station
d a bank   j a town hall
e a marketplace   k a post office
f a pub

a
b
c
d
e
f
g
h
i
j
k

▶ Listening exercise 16

Where do these people want to go?

Wo ist...? *Where is...?*

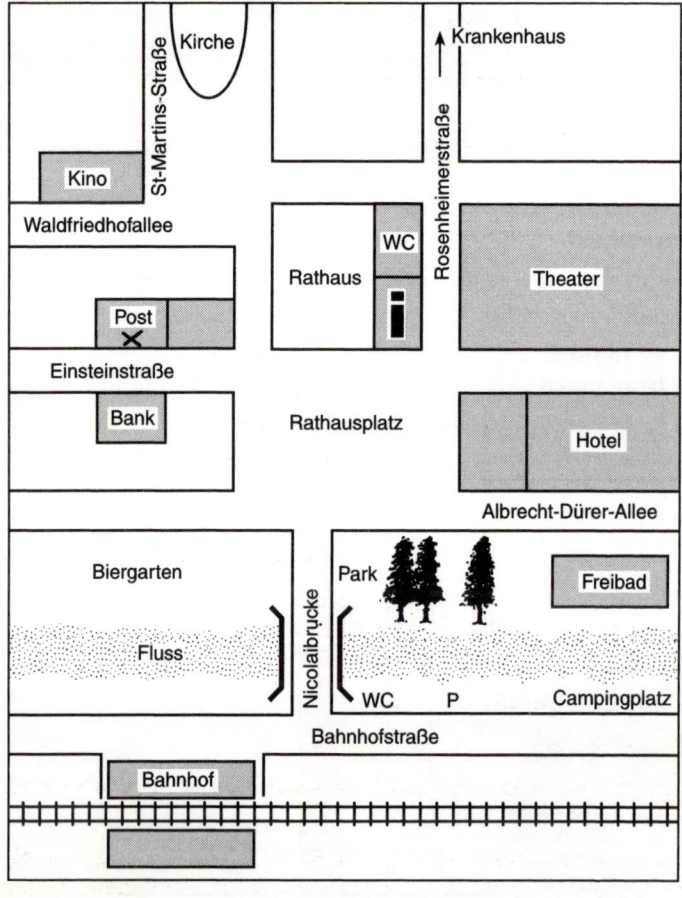

Legende *Key*

die Kirche	die Toiletten	der Park
das Kino	das Informationsbüro	das Hotel
das Theater	der Parkplatz	das Freibad
der Bahnhof	die Post	das Krankenhaus
das Restaurant	die Bank	der Biergarten

Exercise 4

Können Sie die Lücken ausfüllen? *Can you fill the gaps?*

a Das Rathaus ist am ...platz.
b Der Bahnhof ist in der ...straße.
c Die Post ist in der ...straße.
d Das Freibad ist in der ... Allee.
e Die Bank ist in der ...straße.
f Das Restaurant ist am ...platz.
g Das Informationsbüro und die Toiletten sind (are) in der ...straße.
h Das Kino ist in der ...allee.

Exercise 5

Ask where these places are ...

Wo ist hier ein/eine ...? *Where is there a ... (here)?*

a die Kirche
b das Theater
c das Restaurant
d das Informationsbüro
e die Post
f der Park
g das Freibad
h der Biergarten
i das Kino
j der Bahnhof
k die Toilette
l der Parkplatz
m die Bank
n das Hotel
o das Krankenhaus
p der Campingplatz

Now give the full answer (without looking at **Exercise 2** if possible), e.g. Die Kirche ist in der ... Straße.

Word patterns

Trigger words

A trigger word is a word which sometimes changes the word which comes after it.

You might have noticed that the word for street is **die Straße**, but when you say *in the street* it becomes **in der Straße**. This is because the word **in** is a trigger word which sometimes changes **die** to **der**.

    in + die = in der   in der Hauptstraße

In also sometimes changes **der** and **das** to produce **in dem**, and this is almost always shortened to **im**:

    in + der = in dem (im)   im Park
    in + das = in dem (im)   im Hotel

It is the trigger words (or prepositions) that make people think German is a difficult language to learn.

However, it is perfectly possible to speak understandable German without learning all the rules. The best thing is to learn some useful phrases by heart so that you are used to the pattern of the words and then use them as models to build phrases of your own, e.g.

Ich bin im Hotel Stern in der Hauptstraße.
I am at the Star Hotel in the main street.

Then change the name of the hotel and the street as necessary.

Revision

1 Pair up the English and the German words.

a	der Bahnhof	i	the bridge
b	die Bar	ii	the café
c	die Bibliothek	iii	the church
d	die Brücke	iv	the youth hostel
e	das Café	v	the restaurant
f	der Dom	vi	the pub
g	der Flughafen	vii	the library
h	das Informationsbüro	viii	the hospital
i	die Jugendherberge	ix	the cathedral
j	das Kino	x	the town hall
k	die Kirche	xi	the castle
l	die Kneipe	xii	the cinema
m	das Krankenhaus	xiii	the airport
n	der Marktplatz	xiv	the snack bar
o	das Rathaus	xv	the street
p	das Restaurant	xvi	the bar
q	das Schloss	xvii	the station
r	der Schnellimbiss	xviii	the marketplace
s	die Straße	xix	the information office

2 Work out what these words mean by breaking them up (here are a few extra clues: **Haupt** *main*, **Auskunft** *information*, **Stelle** *place*).

der Campingplatz   die Fußgängerzone
die Hauptpost   der Hauptbahnhof

das Auskunftsbüro
die Polizeiwache
die Bushaltestelle
die Autobahnbrücke

der Sportplatz
der Busbahnhof
die Tankstelle
die Landungsbrücke

▶ Listening exercise 17

Richtig oder falsch? *True or false?*

		R	F
a	Die Kirche ist in der Griechstraße.	☐	☐
b	Die Bar ist in der Neustraße.	☐	☐
c	Die Post ist in der Rheinallee.	☐	☐
d	Das Café ist in der Burgstraße.	☐	☐
e	Die Bank ist am Marktplatz.	☐	☐
f	Die Kneipe ist in der Bahnhofstraße.	☐	☐
g	Die Toiletten sind am Parkplatz.	☐	☐
h	Das Informationsbüro ist am Rathausplatz.	☐	☐
i	Der Parkplatz ist in der Bonner Allee.	☐	☐
j	Die Jugendherberge ist am Rheinweg.	☐	☐

Sign language

Which sign is it?

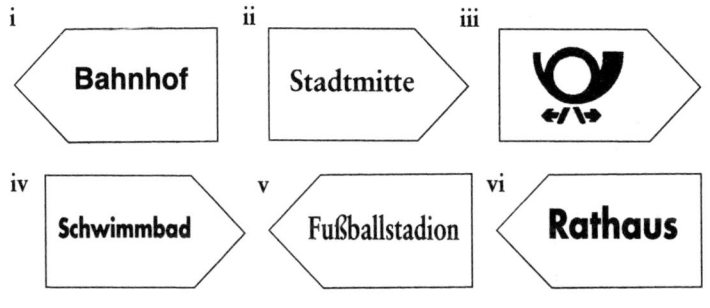

i   Bahnhof
ii   Stadtmitte
iii
iv   Schwimmbad
v   Fußballstadion
vi   Rathaus

a	the football stadium	d	the station
b	the post office	e	the town hall
c	the town centre	f	the swimming pool

09

wie komme ich zur Post?

how do I get to the post office?

In this unit you will learn how to
- ask for directions
- give directions
- ask and say how far somewhere is

Wie komme ich dorthin? *How do I get there?*

Word patterns

Zu is a trigger word which changes | **die** to **der**
| **der** to **dem**
| **das** to **dem**
| **die** (plural) to **den**

Zum is an abbreviation of | **zu + dem.**
Zur is an abbreviation of | **zu + der.**
So with **der** and **das** words you use | **zum: zum** Bahnhof.
With **die** words you use | **zur: zur** Post.
With plural words you use | **zu den: zu den** Toiletten.
Wie komme ich **zum** Bahnhof? | *How do I get to the station?*
| (lit: how come I ...)

zur Post	*to the post office*
zum Rathaus	*to the town hall*

Memorize the phrases **zum Bahnhof, zur Post** and **zu den Toiletten** and use them to remind yourself of the correct forms.

Don't worry – even if you don't get them right, Germans will still be able to understand where you are asking for!

Exercise 1: *zum* or *zur*?

How would you ask the way to these places?

(First decide whether they are der, die, or das words.)

Wie komme ich zu ... a Rathaus?
b Krankenhaus?
c Hotel?
d Café?
e Restaurant?
f Bank?
g Freibad?
h Supermarkt (m)?
i Tankstelle?
j Campingplatz?
k Parkplatz?
l Busbahnhof?

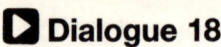 **Dialogue 18**

Sie	Passant
Wie komme ich am besten zur Post?	
	Sie gehen hier geradeaus. Die Post ist auf der rechten Seite.
Vielen Dank. Auf Wiedersehen.	
Wie komme ich am besten zum Freibad?	
	Sie nehmen die erste Straße links. Das Freibad ist auf der linken Seite.
Vielen Dank. Auf Wiedersehen.	
Wie komme ich am besten zum Bahnhof?	
	Sie nehmen die erste Straße rechts und die zweite Straße links.

links/rechts	*left/right*
geradeaus	*straight ahead*
die erste Straße rechts	*the first street right*
die zweite Straße links	*the second street left*
auf der linken Seite	*on the left (side)*
auf der rechten Seite	*on the right (side)*
Sie nehmen ...	*you take ...*
zum/zur	*to the*

Pronunciation tips

ch as in loch
ei as in eye
ge as in grass

Learning note

- Check you understand the German and then practise saying the dialogues.

Exercise 2

Tell your German friend the following directions:

a straight ahead, on the right
b first right, on the left
c second left, on the left
d first left, on the right
e second right, on the right
f straight ahead, on the left

Im Informationsbüro *At the information office*

Gibt es ... in der Nähe?	*Is there a ... near here?*
Ich rufe mal an.	*I'll give them a ring.* (lit: I call just up)
noch	*still*
frei	*free, available*
Einzel- oder Doppelzimmer	*single or double room*
mit Dusche	*with shower*
mit Bad	*with bath*
zu Fuß	*on foot*
mit dem Auto	*(with the) by car*
entlang	*along*
die Einbahnstraße	*one-way street*

Entlang means *along* but instead of saying *along the street* in German it is more correct to say 'the street along': **die Straße entlang.**

Pronunciation tip

Nähe sounds like **nay-er.**

Language notes

	m.	f.	n.
Gibt es	einen Parkplatz?	eine Bank?	ein Hotel?

There are two ways of saying *I go* or *I am going* in German. If you are walking you say: **ich gehe** and if you are driving or being driven you use: **ich fahre**.

Ich fahre	mit dem Auto.	I am going	by car.
	mit dem Bus.		by bus.
	mit dem Zug.		by train.
	mit der Straßenbahn.		by tram.
	mit der U-Bahn.		by underground.

Exercise 3

How do you ask if there is ... near here?

a a station   **e** a bank
b a campsite   **f** a pub
c a post office   **g** a bus stop
d a car park   **h** an hotel

Exercise 4

What would you ask? You want a room with:

a

c

b

d

Exercise 5

How do you say you are travelling:

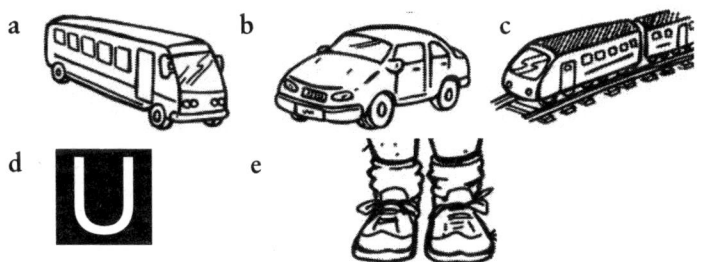

a b c

d e

▶ Dialogue 19

Sie	Empfangsdame
Entschuldigen Sie bitte. Gibt es ein Hotel in der Nähe?	
	Ja. Das Hotel Zur Post.
Haben Sie noch Zimmer frei?	
	Ich rufe mal an. (*Sie telefoniert*) Ja. Einzel- oder Doppelzimmer?
Doppelzimmer.	
	Ja. Mit Bad oder Dusche?
Mit Bad. Wie komme ich zum Hotel?	
	Zu Fuß, oder mit dem Auto?
Zu Fuß.	
	Sie gehen die Hauptstraße entlang, und es ist in der zweiten Straße links auf der rechten Seite.
Vielen Dank. Auf Wiedersehen.	
	Auf Wiedersehen.

Wie komme ich zum
Bahnhof?

Zu Fuß, oder mit dem Auto?

Mit dem Auto.

Sie nehmen die zweite
Straße links und die erste
Straße rechts.
Die erste Straße links ist
eine Einbahnstraße.

Learning notes

- Practise both parts of the dialogue.
- Now adapt the dialogue. You want a single room, and the
  hotel is on the first street on the right, on the left-hand side.

Exercise 6

How do you ask:

a Is there a hotel near here?
b Have they still got rooms available?
c How do I get to the hotel on foot? and by car? and by bus?

Exercise 7

Describe where the destination marked X is in each of these
diagrams (you are standing at point A).

 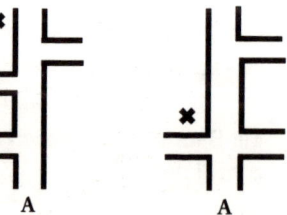

Ist es weit? *Is it far?*

Ist es weit?	*Is it far?*
dort drüben	*over there*
da	*there*
hier vorne	*in front (of you)*
hier hinten	*behind (you)*
gleich hier	*right there*
um die Ecke	*around the corner*
gegenüber	*opposite (trigger word)*
Wo kann ich Briefmarken kaufen?	*Where can I buy stamps?*
Ich weiß es nicht.	*I don't know.*
Ich bin hier fremd.	*I am a stranger here (myself).*

Pronunciation tips

w sounds **v**
d at the end of a word sounds **t**
ei sounds **eye**

i When asked how far away somewhere is, Germans usually reply by telling you how long it takes to get there. **Z.B.** (Zum Beispiel – for example). **Wie weit ist es zum Bahnhof? Fünf Minuten zu Fuß.** *Five minutes on foot.*

Learning notes

- Practise the new words and phrases. Say them out loud.
- Cover up the English and see how many you can understand.
- Decide which you should learn well enough to be able to use, and which you should be able to understand.
- Now cover up the German and see how many you can remember.

Exercise 8

Refer again to the map on page 76.

You are standing in front of the information office. To which building do the following directions refer?

a Gleich hier um die Ecke.
b Gegenüber dem Freibad.
c Nehmen die erste Straße
links und geradeaus.

d Auf der rechten Seite.
e Gleich hier vorne.
f Dort drüben, links.
g Gegenüber der Bank.

▶ Dialogue 20

You are looking for the Frauenkirche in München. Ask this lady:

Sie	Dame
Entschuldigen Sie, bitte. Wo ist die Frauenkirche?	
	Es tut mir Leid. Ich weiß es nicht. Ich bin hier fremd.

So you decide to go into the Informationsbüro instead.

Sie	Dame
Wo ist der Dom?	
	Hier gleich vorne.
Und wo sind die Toiletten?	
	Dort drüben.
Wo ist das Hotel Zum Garten?	
	Hier rechts, geradeaus und dann auf der rechten Seite.
Ist das weit?	
	Nein. Fünf Minuten zu Fuß.
Wo kann ich hier Briefmarken kaufen?	
	Die Post ist hier um die Ecke.
Und wo ist das Rathaus?	
	In der Fußgängerzone. Da, sehen Sie, dort hinten.

Learning notes

- Read the dialogues and make sure you understand everything in them. Which phrases do you know already?
- Look at the new phrases and choose three that you think it would be useful to learn. Write them down in English and see if you can put them back into German.

Exercise 9

Ask where these places are and if they are far:

a post office   **b** station   **c** church   **d** bank   **e** cinema
f hotel   **g** supermarket

Exercise 10

Now it's your turn to give directions. Use the plan to answer the following questions in German.

a Wie komme ich zum Hotel Alpblick?
b Gibt es eine Bank hier in der Nähe?
c Wo kann ich hier Briefmarken kaufen?
d Gibt es ein Kino in der Nähe?
e Wie komme ich zum Bahnhof?
f Wo ist hier ein Restaurant?
g Wie komme ich zum Schloss?
h Ist es weit?

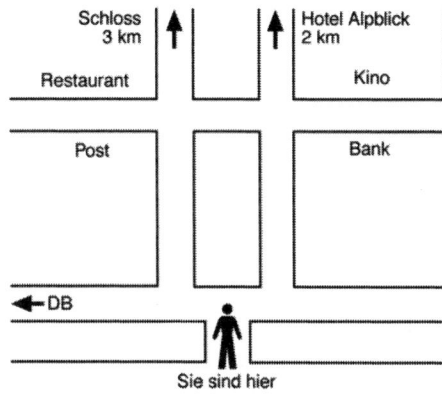

Language notes

In this unit you have met some more trigger words:

auf	[die Seite] **auf** der rechten Seite
mit	[das Auto] **mit** dem Auto
gegenüber	[der Bahnhof] **gegenüber** dem Bahnhof

Revision

1 Can you ask the following:

   a the way to the station?   **d** where there is a bank?
   b is it far?   **e** if there is a hotel nearby?
   c where you can buy stamps?   **f** if it still has rooms free?

2 Check that you can say the following:

   a first on the right   **g** a single room with bath
   b second on the left   **h** a double room with
   c straight ahead   shower
   d around the corner   **i** in a car
   e on the left-hand side   **j** on foot
   f on the right-hand side

3 Do you remember how to say the following?
   a I'm sorry.   **d** Excuse me, please.
   b I don't understand.   **e** Pardon?
   c I don't know.   **f** Thank you.

Sign language

What do these signs mean?

a  Post

b **Bank**   **c** **Rathaus**

d *Kino*   **e** **Hallenbad**

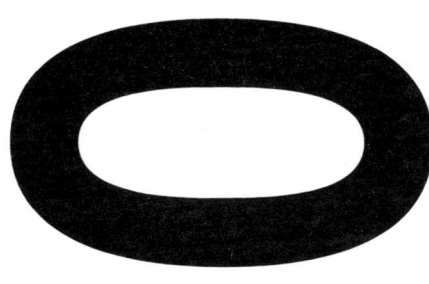

10

der Kalender

the calendar

In this unit you will learn how to
- say the months of the year
- say public holidays, days and dates
- say when your holidays are
- understand an invitation
- invite someone to stay
- make arrangements

▶ Wann kommen Sie? *When are you coming?*

die Monate	the months
Januar [*yan*-oo-ar]	January
Februar [*feb*-roo-ar]	February
März [*meh*-rts]	March
April [a-*pril*]	April
Mai [my]	May
Juni [*yoo*-ny]	June
Juli [*yoo*-ly]	July
August [ow-*gust*]	August
September [zep-*tem*-ber]	September
Oktober [ok-*to*-ber]	October
November [no-*vem*-ber]	November
Dezember [day-*tsem*ber]	December
die Feiertage	public holidays
Sommerferien	summer holidays
Winterferien	winter holidays
Osterferien	Easter holidays
Herbstferien	autumn holidays

Pronunciation tips

The italic parts of the sounds shown in brackets for the months are stressed. Remember also: **j** sounds y (**yuh**).

Learning notes

- Read the names of the months out loud.
- Which month is it? Say out loud the full word for each of these abbreviations:

  Mai Dez Jul   Feb Jun Sept
  Jan Aug Mär Okt Apr Nov

- Which holiday is it?

Wo 1 Januar

1

Donnerstag

Neujahr

Wo 16 April

17

Freitag

Karfreitag

Wo 16 April

19

Sonntag

Ostersonntag

Wo 17 April

20

Montag

Ostermontag

Wo 22 Mai

29

Sonntag

Pfingsten

Wo 52 Dezember

24

Donnerstag

Heiligabend

Wo 52 Dezember

25

Freitag

1. Weihnachtstag

Wo 53 Dezember

31

Donnerstag

Silvester

▶ Dialogue 21

Practise the dialogue.

Sie	Fräulein Schneider
	Wann kommen Sie nach Deutschland?
Ich komme am 14. März.	
	Wie lange bleiben Sie?
Eine Woche.	
	Wann fahren Sie ab?
Am 22. März. Wann kommen Sie nach England?	
	Am 15. Oktober.

Wie lange bleiben Sie?

Zwei Wochen.

Wann fahren Sie ab?

Am 1. November.
Wann kommen Sie zu uns?

Ich komme vom 4. bis zum
7. Juni, wenn das geht.

Ja. Das geht. Ich freue mich
schon darauf.

Wann fahren Sie ab?	*When are you leaving?*
Wie lange bleiben Sie?	*How long are you staying?*
wenn das geht	*if that is all right*

Word patterns

Am ... *On the ...*

am ersten *on the first*
am zweiten *on the second*
am dritten *on the third*
am fünften *on the fifth*
usw. (und so weiter) *etc.*
  (and so on)

am zehnten *on the tenth*
am zwanzigsten *on the
  twentieth*
am einundzwanzigsten
  on the 21st
am dreißigsten *on the 30th*

Vom ... bis zum ... *From ... to ...*

vom 8. Juli bis zum 1. August *from 8 July to 1 August*
(vom achten Juli bis zum ersten August)

an (*on*) is a trigger word and **am** is an abbreviation of **an dem**.
von (*from/of*) is a trigger word and **vom** is an abbreviation of
von dem.

zu (*to*) is a trigger word and **zum** is an abbreviation of **zu dem**.
A trigger word is a word which may change **der** to **dem**.
                                         die to **der**.
                                         das to **dem**.

Eine Einladung *An invitation*

Möchten Sie uns besuchen?	*Would you like to visit us?* (lit: would you like us visit)
Ja, gerne.	*Yes, I would.* (lit: yes, willingly)
Wann können Sie kommen?	*When can you come?*
Ich weiß es nicht.	*I don't know.* (lit: I know it not)
Wann passt es Ihnen?	*When does it suit you?*
genau	*exactly*
nur	*only*
frei	*free*
zu Weihnachten	*at/for Christmas* (lit: to Christmas)
zu Ostern	*at Easter*
Geht das?	*Is that OK?* (lit: goes that?)
Ja, das geht.	*Yes, that's OK.* (lit: yes, that goes)
Ich freue mich schon darauf.	*I'm already looking forward to it.*
Vielen Dank für die Einladung	*Many thanks for the invitation*
Nichts zu danken.	*Don't mention it.*
Auf Wiederhören.	*Goodbye (on the phone).*

Pronunciation tips

v sounds f   ei as eye

ö as ur   au as ow in owl

ge as gue in guest   freue – froy-uh

Learning notes

- Practise reading all the words and phrases out loud (repeating after the recording if you have it).
- Cover up the English and see if you can remember what all the German words and phrases mean.
- Cover up the German and see if you can remember it.
- Count how many words and phrases you know already and choose three new ones to try to learn.

Exercise 1

Saying *thank you*. How do you say the following using the phrases in the box?

a Thank you very much.
b Thanks.
c Many thanks.
d Don't mention it.

i	**Danke schön**	**iii**	**Danke.**
ii	**Nichts zu danken.**	**iv**	**Vielen Dank.**

▶ Dialogue 22

Sie (am Telefon)	Fräulein Hoffman
	Hallo! Wie geht's?
Gut danke. Und Ihnen?	
	Gut. Möchten Sie uns in Deutschland besuchen?
Ja, gerne.	
	Wann können Sie kommen?
Ich weiß nicht. Wann passt es Ihnen?	
	Wann sind die Sommerferien?
Vom 15. Juli bis zum 8. August.	
	Und wann sind die Weihnachtsferien?
Vom 20. Dezember bis zum 3. Januar.	
	Wann sind die Osterferien?
Das weiß ich nicht genau.	
	Ostersonntag ist am 4. April.
Ich habe nur zwei Tage frei.	
	Möchten Sie zu Weihnachten kommen?
Gerne. Ich habe vom 20. bis 28. Dezember frei. Geht das?	

Vielen Dank für die
Einladung.

Ja. Das geht.
Ich freue mich schon darauf.

Nichts zu danken.
Auf Wiederhören.

Auf Wiederhören.

Learning tips

- Read the text carefully and make sure you understand everything.
- Practise reading it out loud. See if you can get someone to read the other part with you.
- Try to substitute the dates of your own holidays. If you don't know them use these:
  Easter: 2–7 April.   Christmas: 23 December – 3 January.
  Summer: 14–30 July.

Wann treffen wir uns? *When shall we meet?*

ins *in + das = ins*	*(in)to the*
nächste Woche	*next week*
nächsten Montag	*next Monday*
morgens	*in the morning*
nachmittags	*in the afternoon*
abends	*in the evening*
heute	*today*
morgen Abend	*tomorrow evening*
Wie wäre es mit Dienstag?	*What about Tuesday?* (lit: how would it be with Tuesday?)
Das geht leider nicht.	*That won't do/I can't make it.* (lit: that goes unfortunately not)
Prima!	*Great!*
keine Zeit	*no time*

Language notes

Das Datum: *the date*

Dates are written like this: **den 14. Juni** *or* **14. 6.**

and read like this: **den vierzehnten Juni** *or*
den vierzehnten sechsten

The full stop after the figure represents **-ten** which is like the English *-th* in *4th, 5th, 10th*, etc, or *-rd* in *23rd*.

Now read these dates out loud remembering to add the **-ten** (or **-sten** if the number is more than 20) wherever there is a full stop.

a 5. März	**d** 10. Feb	**g** 13. 5.	**j** 27. 4.
b 19. Nov	**e** 8. Okt	**h** 7. 9.	**k** 1. 8.
c 21. Jul	**f** 30. Jan	**i** 12. 5.	**l** 28. 10

Wann haben Sie Geburtstag? *When is your birthday?*

Mein Geburtstag ist am … or **Ich habe am … Geburtstag.**

And can you say when the birthdays ringed below are?

JAN
Mo		7	14	21	28
Di	1	8	15	22	29
Mi	2	9	16	23	30
Do	3	10	17	24	(31)
Fr	4	11	18	25	
Sa	5	12	19	26	
So	6	13	20	27	

MAI
Mo		6	13	20	27
Di		7	14	21	28
Mi	1	8	15	22	29
Do	2	9	16	23	30
Fr	3	10	17	24	31
Sa	4	11	18	25	
So	5	12	19	26	

SEPT
Mo		2	9	16	23 30
Di		3	10	17	24
Mi		4	11	18	25
Do		5	12	19	26
Fr		6	13	20	27
Sa		7	14	21	(28)
So	1	8	15	22	29

FEB
Mo		4	11	18	25
Di		5	12	19	26
Mi		6	13	20	27
Do		7	14	21	28
Fr	1	8	15	22	
Sa	2	9	16	23	
So	3	10	17	24	

JUN
Mo		3	10	17	24
Di		4	11	18	25
Mi		5	12	19	26
Do		6	13	20	27
Fr		7	14	21	28
Sa	1	8	15	22	29
So	2	9	(16)	23	30

OKT
Mo		7	14	21	28
Di	1	8	15	22	29
Mi	2	9	16	23	30
Do	3	10	17	24	31
Fr	4	11	18	25	
Sa	5	12	19	26	
So	6	13	20	27	

MÄR
Mo		4	11	18	25
Di		5	12	19	26
Mi		6	13	20	27
Do		7	14	21	28
Fr	1	8	15	22	29
Sa	2	9	16	23	30
So	3	10	17	24	31

JUL
Mo	1	8	15	22	29
Di	2	9	16	23	30
Mi	3	10	17	24	31
Do	4	11	18	25	
Fr	5	12	19	26	
Sa	6	13	20	27	
So	7	14	21	28	

NOV
Mo		4	11	18	25
Di		5	12	19	26
Mi		6	13	(20)	27
Do		7	14	21	28
Fr	1	8	15	22	29
Sa	2	9	16	23	30
So	3	10	17	24	

APR
Mo	1	8	15	22	29
Di	2	9	16	23	30
Mi	3	10	17	24	
Do	4	11	18	25	
Fr	5	12	19	26	
Sa	6	13	20	27	
So	7	14	21	28	

AUG
Mo		5	12	19	26
Di		6	13	20	27
Mi		7	14	21	28
Do	1	8	15	22	29
Fr	2	9	16	23	30
Sa	3	10	17	24	31
So	4	11	18	25	

DEZ
Mo		2	9	16	23 30
Di		3	10	17	24 31
Mi		4	11	18	25
Do		5	12	19	26
Fr		6	(13)	20	27
Sa		7	14	21	28
So	1	8	15	22	29

What date are you arriving and leaving?
Ich komme ... *I'm arriving* ...
Ich fahre ... *I'm going/leaving* ...

e.g. 20. 7.–1. 8.: **Ich komme am zwanzigsten siebten.**
Ich fahre am ersten achten.

a 13.07.–25.07.   c 21.12.–27.12.
b 16.08.   d 4.03.–18.03.

▶ Dialogue 23

Sie	**Herr Braun**
	Gehen wir ins Kino?
Ja, gerne. Wann?	
	Nächste Woche, am Montag?
	Geht das?
Ja. Um wie viel Uhr?	
	Um sieben Uhr abends.

Gehen wir in die Pizzeria?	
	Ja, gerne. Wann?
Morgen Abend?	
	Nein. Das geht leider nicht. Wie wäre es mit Mittwochabend?
Ja, prima. Um wie viel Uhr?	
	Um halb sieben?
Ja, bis dann. Tschüss.	

Spielen wir heute Nachmittag Tennis?	
	Heute habe ich keine Zeit. Wie wäre es mit Samstag?
Ja, gut. Um wie viel Uhr?	
	Um zwei Uhr nachmittags.

Learning note

• Read both parts of the dialogues.

Exercise 2

How would you invite someone to do the following? Note that the day of the week and/or times come earlier in the German sentence:

Example: Go to the theatre with you on Friday evening?
Answer: Gehen wir Freitagabend ins Theater?

a Play tennis with you on Monday evening.
b Go to the cinema with you tomorrow evening.
c Go to the pizzeria with you today at 8pm.

Now use what you have learned to invite someone to:

d Go swimming (**schwimmen**) Wednesday afternoon.
e Play squash Saturday at 11.00.
f Go to a restaurant (**das Restaurant**) Friday evening.

Exercise 3

Frau Fischer invites you to their house that evening. Complete this short conversation.

Fr. Fischer	Kommen Sie heute Abend zu uns?
You	*Say you can't make it tonight.*
Fr. Fischer	Oh, das tut mir Leid.
	Wann können Sie kommen?
You	*Ask if Thursday evening would be all right.*

Exercise 4

Rollenspiel *Role play*

Am Telefon *On the phone:* You are going to visit Herr Braun in Köln. Say your part of the dialogue.

	Herr Braun	Hallo. ... Wie geht's?
a	**You**	*Well, thank you and you?*
	Herr Braun	Gut, danke. Wann kommen Sie?
b	**You**	*On Monday, 15 July.*
	Herr Braun	Wann kommen Sie in Köln an?
		(When do you get in to Cologne?)
c	**You**	*At 18.35.*
	Herr Braun	Wann fahren Sie von London ab?
		(When do you leave London?)
d	**You**	*At 9.30am.*
	Herr Braun	Wie lange bleiben Sie?
		(How long are you staying?)

e	**You**	*Until Friday evening.*
	Herr Braun	Um wie viel Uhr fahren Sie ab?
f	**You**	*At 19.30.*
	Herr Braun	Wann kommen Sie in London an?
g	**You**	*At 7.30am.*
	Herr Braun	Gut. Ich freue mich schon darauf.
h	**You**	*Goodbye.*
	Herr Braun	Auf Wiederhören.

i Germans like to celebrate their birthdays and often take cakes or buns to work to share with their colleagues on their birthday.

If you are giving flowers as a present you should always buy an odd number and unwrap them as you hand them over.

eine Geburtstagskarte　　　　**eine Weihnachtskarte**

Revision

1　Making arrangements. **Wann treffen wir uns?** *When shall we meet?* Tell your friend you will see her on:

　　a　Monday 2 May at 12.30
　　b　Friday 24 December at 14.30
　　c　next Saturday at 11.15
　　d　next week, on Thursday at 16.30
　　e　Wednesday 16 April 9.15
　　f　Saturday 1 September at 17.00
　　g　next Tuesday at 13.30
　　h　Friday at 8pm

▶ Listening exercise 18

Wann treffen wir uns? *When shall we meet?*

Note down the times and dates of these eight meetings.

German verbs

In this unit you will learn how to
- identify a verb
- know which form of the verb to use
- make the correct form of the verb
- talk about what is happening (present tense) and what has happened (past tense)
- look up verbs in the dictionary

This unit does not work in the same way as the preceding and following ones. Do not try to learn everything in it at once. Use it for reference and come back to it as and when you need it.

Verbs are 'doing words': go, sleep, run, eat, talk, think, understand, speak – all things which one can 'do'.

To check if a word is a verb try saying it after:

I ...   *or* I can ...

You can learn to speak a language at a simple and effective level by using phrases which you have learned which already include the verb in its correct form, e.g.

Wie **heißen** Sie?   Ich **wohne** in ...   Wann **treffen** wir uns?

But there will come a time when you want to say something which you haven't learned and you will want to make up a phrase of your own. To do this you need to learn something more about the patterns of the language.

Look at the pattern of a verb in English:

To make (infinitive)			
(singular)		(plural)	
I	make	we	make
you	make	you	make
he/she/it	make**s**	they	make

Now look at the same verb in German:

machen (infinitive)			
(singular)		(plural)	
ich	mach**e**	wir	mach**en**
du	mach**st**	ihr	mach**t**
er/sie/es	mach**t**	sie	mach**en**
		Sie	mach**en**
		(you – polite form)	

It is obviously easier to learn an English verb than a German one, because it is the same as the infinitive except that you add an **s** in the *he/she/it* form. (The infinitive is the form of the verb that you will find if you look it up in a dictionary.)

The German verb has seven forms (or persons):

The **ich** form, **du** form, **er** form, **wir** form, **ihr** form, **sie** form and **Sie** form.

You already know some of them:

    ich form – Ich wohn<u>e</u>, ich heiß<u>e</u>

    du form – Wann komm<u>st</u> du?

    wir form – Wann treff<u>en</u> wir uns?

    Sie form – Wie heiß<u>en</u> Sie?

We are leaving the **ihr** form out for now. So that leaves us with:

    er form   (he/she/it)

    sie form   (they)

Now look at the German verb again and you will find that these two forms are: er/sie/es mach<u>t</u> and sie mach<u>en</u>.

You make the correct form by taking the **-en** off the infinitive – this gives you the 'stem' of the verb – you then add the ending that you need: **-e, -st, -t** or **-en**. Here is a short summary of all the endings:

The **ich** form ends in **-e**	The **wir** form ends in **-en**
	[The **ihr** form ends in **-t**]
The **du** form ends in **-st**	The **sie** form ends in **-en**
The **er** form ends in **-t**	The **Sie** form ends in **-en**

Exercise 1

a I eat (I am eating) … I am called … I live …

    You are talking about yourself so what will the verb end with?

b What is your name? Where do you live (*you* – polite form)?

    You are talking to a stranger so what will the verb end with?

c What is your name? Would you like a cup of coffee?

    You are talking to a younger person so what will the verb end with?

d You are talking about yourself and someone else (John and I …). Which form will you use? What will the verb end with?

Word patterns

When you are talking about yourself in German the verb almost always ends with an **-e** although it is not always pronounced clearly in spoken German. Remember: **ich** form: **ich …e**

What is the ich form of these verbs?

infinitive		ich form	
haben	to *have*	**ich**	I have
spielen	to *play*	**ich**	I play
machen	to *make*	**ich**	I make
gehen	to *go*	**ich**	I go
schwimmen	to *swim*	**ich**	I swim
essen	to *eat*	**ich**	I eat
trinken	to *drink*	**ich**	I drink
fahren	to *drive*	**ich**	I drive
sehen	to *see*	**ich**	I see
kommen	to *come*	**ich**	I come

If you know the infinitive it is easy, but what happens when you don't know the word you need? You look it up in the dictionary.

You want to say you will *fetch* the book, so you look up the word *fetch* in the dictionary and this is what it says:

    fetch [fetʃ] vt **holen;** (in sale) **einbringen, erzielen.**

The word in brackets [fetʃ] is the phonetic pronunciation of the English word *fetch*. You know how to pronounce it already so you can ignore this.

You don't want to say how much something fetches in a sale so you can ignore all the second part; the word you want is **holen.**

holen is the infinitive, so what is the **ich** form going to be?

holen to *fetch*   **ich hole** I *fetch*

Try it again. You want to say I'll *bring* the book.
Look up *to bring*:

    bring [briŋ] vt. irreg. **bringen;** – about **zustande bringen ...**

From 'vt.' you know that it is a verb; 'irreg.' tells you that it is an irregular verb; **bringen** tells you the infinitive of the verb that you want, so you can ignore the rest of the text.

bringen is the infinitive, so the **ich** form will be **ich bringe.**

The present tense

You use the present tense to say what you are doing now (or do regularly).

Talking about yourself (I)

Use the **ich** form, ending in **-e**.

I go	*or* I am going	**ich gehe**
I eat	*or* I am eating	**ich esse**
I drink	*or* I am drinking	**ich trinke**
I go/drive	*or* I am going/driving	**ich fahre**

gehen means to go when you go on foot; **fahren** is used if you go by transport.

Talking about yourself and someone else (we)

Use the **wir** form, ending in **-en**.

we go	*or* we are going	**wir gehen**
we eat	*or* we are eating	**wir essen**
we drink	*or* we are drinking	**wir trinken**
we/go drive	*or* we are going/driving	**wir fahren**

Talking about one other person (he or she)

Use the **er/sie** form, ending it **-t**.

he/she goes	*or* he/she is going	**er/sie geht**
he/she eats	*or* he/she is eating	**er/sie isst**
he/she drinks	*or* he/she is drinking	**er/sie trinkt**
he/she goes/drives	*or* he/she is going/driving	**er/sie fährt**

essen and **fahren** are irregular verbs which don't always follow the normal pattern.

Talking about more than one other person (they)

Use the **sie** form, ending in **-en**.

they go	*or* they are going	**sie gehen**
they eat	*or* they are eating	**sie essen**
they drink	*or* they are drinking	**sie trinken**
they go/drive	*or* they are going/driving	**sie fahren**

Using the *du* and *Sie* forms

Remember the normal form is the Sie form.

You use the **du** form only with people you know well and younger people.

Exercise 2

Which forms are you going to use?

a You are talking about your friend Harry.
b You are talking about yourself and Monika.
c You are talking about your friends Herr and Frau Schulz.
d You are asking Herr Braun a question.
e You are asking his young son a question.
f You are talking about yourself.

Language notes

There are some special verbs which don't end in -e in the **ich** form. They are.

ich **weiß**	*I know*	ich **will**	*I want to*
ich **bin**	*I am*	ich **darf**	*I may*
ich **kann**	*I can*	ich **soll**	*I should*
ich **mag**	*I like*		

Word patterns: regular verbs and irregular verbs

Regular verbs are ones which follow a special pattern. Unfortunately, there are also some irregular verbs which don't always follow the pattern.

Present tense

(What you are doing now or usually do)

English has two forms of the present tense, for example:

I play/I am playing   I go/I am going

German only has one, so:

Ich spiele means	*I play* as well as	*I am playing*
Ich gehe means	*I go* as well as	*I am going*

Past tense

(What you have done or what you did in the past)

Past:	I played	I went
Perfect:	I have played	I have gone

If you were learning English verbs you would have to learn, for example:

Regular verbs			**Irregular verbs**		
Infinitive	Past	Past participle	Infinitive	Past	Past participle
play	played	played	go	went	gone
dance	danced	danced	bring	brought	brought
clean	cleaned	cleaned	drink	drank	drunk
wash	washed	washed	eat	ate	eaten
			swim	swam	swum
			come	came	came

The first column is the infinitive, the second is the past tense and the third is the past participle (the part used after *have* in forming the perfect tense: *I have played*). Another way of talking about what you did in the past in English is to say, *I was playing, I was going*; this is known as the imperfect tense.

Here are the same verbs in German. Can you work out which is which?

Infinitive	Past (Imperfect)	Past participle
trinken	trank	getrunken
waschen	wusch	gewaschen
schwimmen	schwamm	geschwommen
kommen	kam	gekommen
*tanzen	tanzte	getanzt
essen	aß	gegessen
gehen	ging	gegangen
bringen	brachte	gebracht
*spielen	spielte	gespielt
*putzen	putzte	geputzt

*These verbs are regular.

Now what do you think these verbs might mean?

singen	sang	gesungen
halten	hielt	gehalten
fallen	fiel	gefallen
finden	fand	gefunden

Forming the past tense in German

This is the pattern of a regular verb in German:

1	2	3	4
Infinitive	**Present** *er* **form**	**Imperfect** *ich/er* **form**	**Past participle**
mach<u>en</u>	mach<u>t</u>	mach<u>te</u>	<u>ge</u>mach<u>t</u>

How to use the table

1 The first column tells you the infinitive of the verb.

2 The second column tells you the **er** form in the present tense because the **du** and **er** forms are sometimes irregular. In the case of this verb it is what you would expect: **-t**.

3 The third column tells you how to form the imperfect tense – how to say: I was doing/I was making. **Ich machte.** (The imperfect tense is usually used to say what was happening when something else happened e.g. I was doing it when I cut myself/I was driving when I hit the wall. It is an 'imperfect' or 'interrupted' action.)

4 The fourth column tells you the past participle of the verb. You need the past participle to make the perfect tense. You add the past participle to *I have* … **Ich habe gemacht.**

> *I did it/have done it.*　　　　**Ich habe es gemacht.**
> *I played/have played tennis.*　　**Ich habe Tennis gespielt.**

Notice how the past participle goes to the end of the phrase.

The **perfect tense** is the one that you use most when talking about what you have done. This is the past tense that you should try to learn first.

Word patterns for past participles

The past participle of a regular verb is made by adding **ge-** to the front of the word and using the **-t** ending:

machen	**ge** + mach + **t**	**gemacht** *made/did*
kaufen	**ge** + kauf + **t**	**gekauft** *bought*

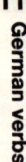

If you are looking up a word which begins with **ge-** in the dictionary and can't find it, it is probably a past participle. Try taking off the **ge-** and looking for the rest of the word.

Exercise 3

What are the infinitives of these verbs? i.e. what should you look up?

a geholt	**c** gearbeitet	**e** gesagt
b gelernt	**d** gefragt	**f** getanzt

Exercise 4

How would you make the past participle of these verbs?

a hören	**c** führen	**e** haben
b brauchen	**d** spielen	**f** kochen

Irregular verbs

Since most of the verbs in common use are irregular ones (just as in English – and they are usually the same ones as in English as our languages have some of the same origins) there is a list of them in most dictionaries and textbooks.

There is a list of the most useful ones on page 220 of this book.

This is how irregular verbs are shown in most dictionaries:

1 Infinitive	2 Present	3 Imperfect	4 Past participle
beginnen	beginnst/beginnt	begann	begonnen – to begin
*bleiben	bleibst/bleibt	blieb	geblieben – to stay
denken	denkst/denkt	dachte	gedacht – to think
essen	isst/isst	aß	gegessen – to eat
fahren	fährst/fährt	fuhr	gefahren – to go/drive

[In this case column 2 includes the **du** and the **er** forms]

How to use the table

1 The infinitive: **beginnen** *to begin*.

2 The present tense: **beginnst/beginnt**. This is what you would expect for the **du** and **er** forms so you know that **beginnen** is regular in the present tense.

3 The imperfect tense: **ich begann** *I began/I was beginning*.

4 The past participle (use with **ich habe: ich habe begonnen** *I began/I have begun*).

bleiben

1 The infinitive: **bleiben** *to stay, to remain.*

2 The present tense: (regular) **du bleibst, er bleibt.**

3 The imperfect: **ich blieb** *I stayed/I was staying* The vowels have changed round: **ei** to **ie.**

4 The past participle **ich bin geblieben** *I stayed/I have stayed.*

*The asterisk tells you to use **ich bin** instead of **ich habe:** *I have stayed* **ich bin** geblieben.

Exercise 5

What is the infinitive of these words? (i.e. what would you look up to find out what these words mean?):

a gelesen	**c** geschlafen	**e** gesehen	**g** gewaschen
b gegeben	**d** gerufen	**f** gefahren	

Using *sein* and *haben* for the perfect tense

The verbs *to be* and *to have* are called auxiliary verbs as they are used as 'helper' verbs to make other tenses.

The present tense of sein and haben

sein *to be*			
ich bin	*I am*	**wir sind**	*we are*
du bist	*you are*	**ihr seid**	*you are*
er/sie/es ist	*he/she/it is*	**sie sind**	*they are*
		Sie sind	*you are (polite form)*

haben *to have*	
ich habe	**wir haben**
du hast	**ihr habt**
er/sie/es hat	**sie haben**
	Sie haben

Sein and **haben** are both used to make the perfect tense:

Ich **habe** Squash **gespielt.**	Ich **bin** in Hamburg **geblieben.**
Ich **habe** den Film **gesehen.**	Ich **bin** nach Köln **gefahren.**
Er **hat** Tennis **gespielt.**	Sie **ist** in München **geblieben.**
Wir **haben** 007 **gesehen.**	Wir **sind** nach Italien **gefahren.**

Remember: You are not supposed to learn everything in this unit at once. Only refer to it as and when you need it.

The main points to remember:

If you are talking about yourself use the **ich** form: after **ich** the verb ends in **-e**:

    e.g. <u>Ich</u> trink<u>e</u> ein Glas Bier.   *I'm drinking a glass of beer.*

If you are saying what you have done use: **Ich habe/ich bin** + the past participle.

Learn this sentence as a model.

Ich bin in die Stadt gefahren und ich habe einen Pullover gekauft.
I went to town and bought a pullover.
(lit: I am in to the town gone and I have a pullover bought)

12 meine Familie
my family

In this unit you will learn how to
- talk about your family
- make plural forms
- say what people are like
- say what your job is
- say what jobs other people do

Meine Familie *My family*

meine Verwandten	*my relations*
mein ...	*my ...*
mein Vater	*my father*
mein Vati	*my dad*
mein Stiefvater	*my stepfather*
mein Schwiegervater	*my father-in-law*
mein Großvater	*my grandfather*
mein Opa	*my grandad*
mein Urgroßvater	*my great-grandfather*
mein Bruder	*my brother*
mein Sohn	*my son*
mein Onkel	*my uncle*
mein Patenonkel	*my godfather*
mein Cousin	*my cousin (male)*
mein Mann	*my husband*
mein Freund	*my friend (male)*
meine ...	*my ...*
meine Mutter	*my mother*
meine Mutti	*my mum*
meine Stiefmutter	*my step-mother*
meine Schwiegermutter	*my mother-in-law*
meine Großmutter	*my grandmother*
meine Oma	*my grandma*
meine Urgroßmutter	*my great-grandmother*
meine Schwester	*my sister*
meine Tochter	*my daughter*
meine Tante	*my aunt*
meine Patentante	*my godmother*
meine Cousine	*my cousin (female)*
meine Frau	*my wife*
meine Freundin	*my friend (female)*

Pronunciation tips

Cousin [cooseng], Cousine [cooseenuh]
ie = ee, ei = eye, ur- sounds oor
w sounds v, Sohn sounds zone

Word patterns

To say *my father* you use **mein** Vater;
to say *my mother* you use **meine** Mutter;
to say *my parents* you say **meine** Eltern.

Use **mein** with masculine (and neuter) words
    meine with feminine words and with plural words.

Learning note

• Choose the words you will need to talk about your family
and try to learn them.

Exercise 1

How do you say the following?

a my father	**i** my wife
b my sister	**j** my husband
c my grandfather	**k** my son
d my parents	**l** my daughter
e my girlfriend	**m** my grandma
f my mother	**n** my grandad
g my brother	**o** my mother-in-law
h my grandmother	

▶ Dialogue 24

Herr Fischer introduces you to his family:

Sie	Herr Fischer
	Darf ich Ihnen meine Frau vorstellen?
Sehr angenehm.	
	Und das ist meine Tochter Angelika.
Hallo, Angelika.	
	Mein Sohn Peter.
Hallo, Peter.	
	Und das ist meine Mutter.
Guten Tag, Frau Fischer.	

And you introduce Herr Fischer to your boss:

Darf ich Ihnen meinen Chef vorstellen?	
Herr Smith – Herr Fischer.	
	Sehr angenehm.
Haben Sie eine gute Reise gehabt?	
	Ja, danke.

> **Haben Sie eine gute Reise gehabt?** *Did you have a good journey?*

▶ Listening exercise 19

Hannelore, Joachim and Katrin describe their family holiday photos. Which relatives are in the photos? Cross out the ones they mention.

a Vater Mutter Großmutter Großvater Bruder Schwester
  Sohn Tochter Hund

b Vater Mutter Großmutter Großvater Bruder Schwester
  Sohn Tochter Hund

c Vater Mutter Großmutter Großvater Bruder Schwester
  Sohn Tochter Hund

Exercise 2

Darf ich meine Familie vorstellen? May I introduce my family? Tell your friend Uschi who these people are!
Hier ist …

Word patterns

If you have more than one …

singular	*plural*
mein Bruder	meine Brüder
meine Schwester	meine Schwestern
mein Sohn	meine Söhne
meine Tochter	meine Töchter

The changes needed to make the plural form are usually shown in brackets after the noun in the vocabulary or in a dictionary, for example:

- **der Bruder** (¨) means that you add an Umlaut to the u to form the plural: **zwei Brüder**.
- **die Schwester (n)** means that you add an 'n' to form the plural: **eine Schwester, zwei Schwestern**.
- **das Fenster (-)** [window] means that the word doesn't change in the plural: ein Fenster, zwei Fenster.

In most dictionaries, if you want to find the plural form you will have to look up the word in the singular in the German–English section; it will not be listed in the English–German section.

Exercise 3

How do you make the plurals of these words?

a die Tochter (¨) *daughter*
b der Tisch (e) *table*
c der Stuhl (¨e) *chair*
d das Haus (¨er) *house*

Leute beschreiben *Describing people*

ziemlich	*rather*
ganz	*quite*
sehr	*very*
nett	*nice*
groß/klein	*big/small*
lang/kurz	*long/short*
hell/dunkel	*light/dark*
schlank/dick	*thin/fat*
schulterlang	*shoulder length*
lockig	*curly*
blau	*blue*

grün	*green*
grau	*grey*
weiß	*white*
rot	*red*
schwarz	*black*
braun	*brown*
Mein Mann ist ziemlich groß.	*My husband is rather tall.*
Meine Frau ist ganz klein.	*My wife is quite small.*
45 Jahre alt	*45 years old*
sehr nett	*very nice*
Er/sie trägt eine Brille.	*He/she wears glasses.*
Kontaktlinsen	*contact lenses*
Er/sie hat blaue/grüne/	*He/she has blue/green/brown*
braune Augen.	*eyes.*
Er hat eine Glatze.	*He is bald.*
gefärbte Haare	*coloured/dyed hair*

Pronunciation tips

ziemlich – [tseemlich]   **klein** – [kline]
e at the end of a word is always pronounced and sounds -uh

Word patterns

Descriptive words (adjectives) all add an **-e** when used in front of a plural word. **Haare** is frequently plural in German (unless you literally mean a single hair), so the adjectives describing someone are plural too, with an **-e**.

Er	hat	lange	blonde	Haare
Sie		kurze	dunkle	
		schulterlange	lockige	

i German people usually know exactly how tall they are and will usually tell you they are 1,74m etc. rather than say ganz groß. Find out how tall you are (in metric measurements!) and learn to say it in German.

Exercise 4

Wie sehen sie aus? Tick the correct statements:

a

i   Er ist groß.
ii Er ist klein.
iii Er hat lange Haare.
iv Er hat kurze Haare.
v   Er trägt eine Brille.
vi Er hat dunkle Haare.
vii Er hat blonde Haare.

b

i   Sie ist groß.
ii Sie ist klein.
iii Sie hat lange Haare.
iv Sie hat kurze Haare.
v   Sie trägt eine Brille.
vi Sie hat dunkle Haare.
vii Sie hat blonde Haare.

Was sind Sie von Beruf? *What job do you do?*

Was sind Sie von Beruf?	*What job do you do?* (lit: what are you by job?)
der Beruf	*job*
arbeiten	*to work*
Ich arbeite (als) ...	*I work as ...*
Ich bin/er ist/sie ist	*I am/he is/she is*
Ich bin selbständig.	*I am self-employed.*
der Lehrer	*teacher*

der Student	student
der Ingenieur	engineer
der Kfz-Mechaniker	car mechanic
der Verkäufer	salesman
der Polizist	policeman
der Zahnarzt	dentist
der Arzt	doctor
der Politiker	politician
der Programmierer	computer programmer
der Schauspieler	actor
der Moderator	radio/TV presenter
der Kellner	waiter
der Vertreter	sales rep
der Angestellte	the employee
der Beamte	the official
der Arbeiter	the worker

Word patterns

All the above 'job' words make the feminine form by adding -**in**, e.g.: der Sekretär, die Sekretär**in**; **Arzt** also adds an Umlaut: der Arzt, die Ärztin.

Note that some jobs end in -**mann**. These usually change their ending to -**frau** if the person is a woman, and to -**leute** if there is more than one:

der Mann – *man* die Frau – *woman*
der Geschäftsmann die Geschäftsfrau *businessman/woman*
der Kaufmann die Kauffrau *buyer/salesperson*
die Leute – *people*
die Geschäftsleute – *business people*
also:
der Frisör/Friseur die Frisörin *hairdresser*

An -**in** ending usually means that a word is feminine.
Der Freund is a friend (male); **die Freundin** is a (female) friend.
der Journalist is a male journalist, so a female one is **die Journalistin**.

Learning notes

- Read the words out loud.
- Select the ones which you think you would find most useful and learn them.

▶ Dialogue 25 Ich bin ... *I am ...*

Sie	Fräulein Fischer
	Was sind Sie von Beruf?
Ich bin Autoelektriker.	
	Was ist Fräulein Smith von Beruf?
Sie ist Krankenschwester.	
	Und was macht Herr Black?
Er ist Kfz-Mechaniker.	
	Was machen Herr und Frau Shaw?
Er ist Elektriker und sie hilft ihm im Geschäft.	
	Was macht ihre Tochter?
Sie ist Buchhändlerin. Sie arbeitet bei einer kleinen Firma.	
	Was macht ihr Sohn?
Er ist Grafiker, aber er ist im Moment arbeitslos.	

Learning notes

- Read the dialogue out loud.
- There are some new words:

  a Krankenschwester **c** Buchhändlerin
  b Elektriker **d** Grafiker

Cross out the ones you already know or can guess. See how many of the clues you need to get the other ones!

a **Kranken** *the sick*, **Schwester** *sister*, so
Krankenschwester *a nurse* (female)
b **der Elektriker** *electrician*
c **das Buch** *the book*
handeln *to trade*, so
der Buchhändler/die Buchhändlerin *bookseller*
d **der Grafiker** *graphic designer*

- Now re-read the dialogue substituting your family or friends and saying what jobs they do.

arbeiten	*to work*
Ich arbeite als ...	*I work as a ...*
der Arbeiter/-in	*worker*
arbeitslos	*without work (unemployed)*
der Arbeitgeber	*employer* (lit: *work giver*)
der Arbeitnehmer	*employee* (lit: *work taker*)
das Arbeitsamt	*employment exchange*
das Amt	*office*

Word patterns

Talking about yourself – the verb ends with -e:
I work   ich arbeit<u>e</u>

Talking about other people – the verb ends with -t:
he works   er arbeite<u>t</u>
she works   sie arbeite<u>t</u>

Talking about yourself and someone else -en:
we work   wir arbeit<u>en</u>

Talking about two or more people -en:
they work   sie arbeit<u>en</u>

Word building

Arbeit(s-) means work   **die Kleidung** means *clothes*
                                   der Platz means ?

So, using the word-building principle it's easy to work out how you would say work clothes and workplace: **die Arbeitskeidung, der Arbeitsplatz.**

Remember that the gender of the new noun is the same as that of the last word.

Exercise 5

What new words can you make with Arbeits- and these words?

a der Beginn *beginning*   **f** die Zeit *time*
b die Pause *break*   **g** die Woche *week*
c das Zimmer *room*   **h** der Schluss *end*
d das Ende *end*   **i** der Vertrag *contract*
e der Tisch *table*

Exercise 6

Using the following vocabulary clues, can you make the German equivalents of the English a–d?

die Post *post*　　　　　**das Amt** *office*
Verkauf- *sales*　　　　**das Büro** *office*
Reise- *travel*　　　　　**Auskunfts-** *information*

a sales office
b information office
c post office
d travel agency

Exercise 7

Look at the pictures of Herr Braun and Silke Müller. Which questions would be suitable to ask each of them, and which replies belong to which person?

a Was sind Sie von Beruf?　　f Was bist du ...?
b Was machst du?　　　　　　g Ich bin Studentin.
c Wo arbeitest du?　　　　　　h Bei BMW.
d Wo arbeiten Sie?　　　　　　i Ich bin Kfz-Mechaniker.
e Was machen Sie?　　　　　　j Auf einer Hotelfachschule.

▶ Listening exercise 20

What do these eight people do for a living?

13

einkaufen
shopping

In this unit you will learn how to
- find your way around the shops
- buy presents and souvenirs
- buy clothes
- ask about sizes, materials and colours
- ask to try something on

Die Läden *The shops*

das Geschäft*	*shop (or business)*
der Laden*	*shop*
die Apotheke	*(dispensing) chemist*
die Buchhandlung	*bookshop*
die Drogerie	*chemist* (not dispensing)
das Elektrogeschäft	*electrical goods*
das Fotogeschäft	*photographer's*
der Geschenkladen	*gift shop*
der Gemüseladen	*greengrocer's*
das Kaufhaus	*department store*
die Reinigung	*cleaner's*
der Schreibwarenladen	*stationer's*
das Schuhgeschäft	*shoe shop*
der Souvenirladen	*souvenir shop*
der Tante-Emma-Laden	*corner shop* (lit: Aunt Emma's shop)
der Zeitungskiosk	*newspaper shop*
Wo ist hier ein Supermarkt?	*Is there a supermarket near here?* (lit. Where is here a supermarket?)
Ausverkauf	*sale*
Zu Verkaufen	*for sale (lit. to sell)*
der Winterschlussverkauf	*winter sales*
der Sommerschlussverkauf	*summer sales*
die Bäckerei	*bakery*
die Konditorei	*cake shop*
der Supermarkt	*supermarket*
das Blumengeschäft	*florist*
die Metzgerei	*butcher's* (South Germany)
der Schlachter	*butcher/butcher's* (North Germany)
der Tabakhändler	*tobacconist*

*These two words for *shop* are often interchangeable.

Exercise 1
Which shop would you go to?

a 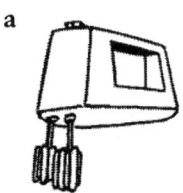   b 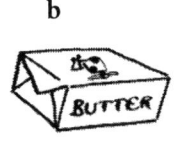   c

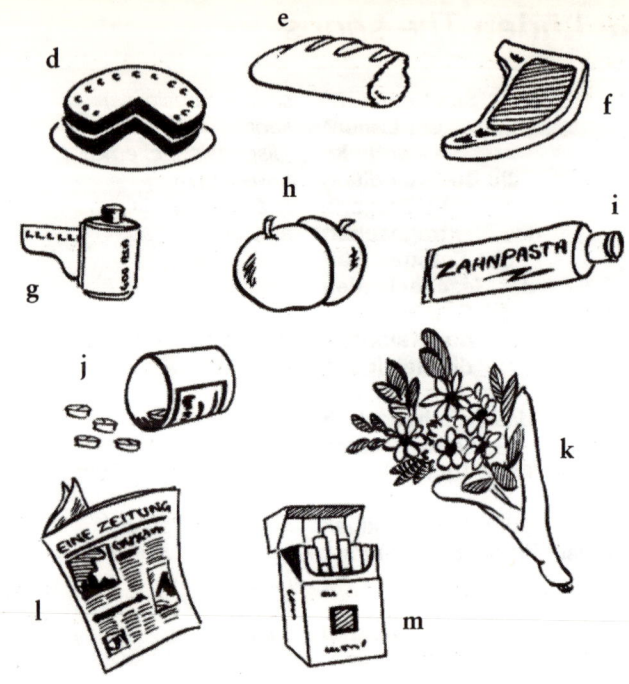

Wo kann ich hier ... kaufen? *Where can I buy ...?*

Briefpapier/Schreibpapier	*writing paper*
ein Buch	*a book*
eine CD/Compact Disc	*a compact disc*
Medikamente	*medicine*
ein Paar Schuhe	*a pair of shoes*
eine Zahnbürste	*a toothbrush*
eine Flasche Parfüm	*a bottle of perfume*
eine Flasche Wein	*a bottle of wine*

Andenken	*souvenirs*	**Blumen**	*flowers*
Briefmarken	*stamps*	**Brot**	*bread*
einen Film	*a film*	**ein Geschenk**	*a present*
einen Kuchen	*a cake*	**einen Mantel**	*a coat*
Zahnpasta	*toothpaste*	**Zigaretten**	*cigarettes*
Weingläser	*wine glasses*	**einen Bierkrug**	*a beer mug*
einen Schal	*a scarf*	**Ohrringe**	*earrings*

Exercise 2

What do you think they might be buying? Fill in a suitable word and then practise the dialogues.

(**Passantin** *passerby*)

Touristin	Wo kann ich hier einen (**a**) ... kaufen?
Passantin	Das Fotogeschäft ist hier gleich um die Ecke.
Touristin	Ich möchte eine (**b**) ... Gibt es ein Musikgeschäft hier in der Nähe?
Touristin	Wo kann ich (**c**) ...... kaufen?
Passantin	Die Post ist in der Hauptstraße neben dem Bahnhof. Aber es gibt einen Zeitungskiosk gleich hier.
Touristin	Ich brauche (**d**) ......
Passantin	Die Drogerie ist neben der Bäckerei.

i As well as at the post office you can usually buy stamps anywhere that sells picture postcards and at most newsagents and tobacconists (who usually sell tickets for local transport).

In an **Apotheke** you can get a prescription made up, but you can also buy medication without a prescription and the **Apotheker** is qualified to suggest remedies for most minor ailments.

Im Geschäft *In the shop*

Ich suche ...	*I am looking for ...*
Wie viel kostet ...?	*How much does ... cost?*
etwa	*about*
Haben Sie etwas Billigeres?	*Have you anything cheaper?*
Kann ich Ihnen helfen?	*Can I help you?*
Sonst noch etwas?	*Anything else?*
ein Geschenk für	*a present for*
ein Geschenk für meinen Mann/meine Frau	*a present for my husband/wife*
ein Geschenk für meinen Bruder/meine Schwester	*a present for my brother/sister*
ein Geschenk für meinen Vater/meine Mutter	*a present for my father/mother*
ein Geschenk für meinen Freund/meine Freundin	*a present for my friend, boyfriend/girlfriend*
ein Geschenk für meinen Sohn/meine Tochter	*a present for my son/daughter*

Könnten Sie es/sie als Geschenk einpacken?	Could you wrap it/them as a present?
Sie bezahlen an der Kasse.	You pay at the cash desk.
Haben Sie eine Tüte, bitte?	Have you a carrier bag, please?
Das reicht, danke.	That's enough, thank you.

Haben Sie ...? *Have you ...?*	**Ich möchte...** *I would like ...*
Ich nehme ... *I'll take ...*	**Ich brauche ...** *I need ...*

Exercise 3

You want to buy presents for your family and friends. How would you say *I am looking for a present for ...?*
Ich suche ein Geschenk für ...

a my girlfriend
b my brother
c my grandmother
d my wife

e my husband
f my mother
g my boyfriend
h my son

Exercise 4

a Ask if they have:
  i a book
  ii writing paper
  iii a bottle of perfume

b Say you're looking for:
  i a bottle of wine
  ii wineglasses
  iii a beer mug

c Say you'd like:
  i a scarf
  ii earrings
  iii a cake

i A gift-wrapping service is offered free in most German shops. You will usually be asked:

Soll ich das als Geschenk einpacken?	*Shall I gift-wrap it for you?*
Soll ich den Preis abmachen?	*Shall I take the price off?*

▶ Dialogue 26

Sie	Verkäuferin
	Kann ich Ihnen helfen?
Ich möchte ein Geschenk für meine Tochter.	
	Wie alt ist sie?
Zwei Jahre.	
	Wie wäre es mit einem Stofftier?
Wieviel kosten sie?	
	Von etwa €25 bis €100.
Wieviel kostet der Teddybär?	
	Der kleine Bär kostet €22, und der große kostet €45,50. Der Hund kostet €48 und die Katze €36.
Ich nehme die Stoffkatze. Könnten Sie es als Geschenk einpacken?	
	Ja, natürlich. Sonst noch etwas?
Haben Sie Computerspiele?	
	Ja. Skifahrer – das ist neu.
Wieviel kostet es?	
	€43.
Haben Sie etwas Billigeres?	
	Ja, Autocops. €18.
Ich nehme es.	
	Sonst noch etwas?
Nein, danke, das ist alles. Was macht das?	
	€54.
Bitte schön.	
	Danke. Auf Wiedersehen.
Auf Wiedersehen.	

  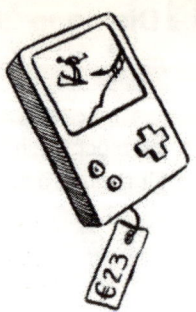

Learning tips

- Read the dialogue and make sure you understand everything.
- Read it out loud then cover up the left-hand side and improvise your part of the dialogue to fit.

▶ **Listening exercise 21**

What are these six customers buying, and for whom?

ℹ️ **Plastikgeld**: Although paying by credit card is becoming more acceptable in Germany, in some restaurants this is still not the case. The most widely used cards are Visa and Eurocard.

Im Kaufhaus *In the department store*

Ich möchte .../Haben Sie ... *I would like .../Have you ...*

einen Pullover	*a jumper*
eine Hose	*trousers* (lit: a trouser)
einen Schal	*a scarf*
ein Paar Handschuhe	*a pair of gloves*
einen Anzug	*a suit*
einen Schlafanzug	*pyjamas* (lit: a sleeping suit)
ein Kleid	*a dress*
einen Jogginganzug	*a track suit*
einen Badeanzug	*a swim suit*
einen Mantel	*a coat*

einfarbig	*plain* (lit: one-coloured)
aus ...	*made of ...*
aus Wolle	*made of wool*
aus Baumwolle	*made of cotton*
aus Leder	*made of leather*
aus Seide	*made of silk*
die Größe	*size*
eine Bluse Größe 36	*a blouse size 36*
das ist zu teuer	*that's too expensive*
Ich nehme es/sie	*I'll take it/them*
Was für ...?	*What kind of ...?*

einen Schlips *a tie*		**ein Hemd** *a shirt*
eine Bluse *a blouse*		**einen Rock** *a skirt*

die Farben *colours*

rot *red*		**rosa(rot)** *pink*
blau *blue*		**grün** *green*
grau *grey*		**schwarz** *black*
weiß *white*		**dunkelblau** *dark blue*
hellblau *light blue*		**türkis** *turquoise*
violett *purple*		**gelb** *a yellow*
braun *brown*		**bunt** *colourful*
gemustert *patterned*		**kariert** *check*
gestreift *striped*		

Learning note

- Read all the new words out loud. Select the ones you think would be the most useful to you and learn them.

Exercise 5

How would you ask for:

a a blue jumper size 38?
b a red blouse size 34?
c a pair of brown trousers size 36?
d a green wool scarf?
e a pair of black gloves?
f a white cotton shirt?

Women's coats,	German	38	40	42	44	46	48	
suits, dresses,	British	10	12	14	16	18	20	
and blouses	American	6	8	10	12	14	16	
	Italian	44	46	48	50	52	54	
	French	40	42	44	46	48	50	
Women's shoes	British	3	4	5	6	7	8	9
	American	4½	5½	6½	7½	8½	9½	10½
	Continental	36	37	38	39	40	41	42
Men's coats,	British	34	36	38	40	42	44	
jackets and	American	34	36	38	40	42	44	
suits	Continental	44	46	48	50	52	54	
Men's shoes	British	6	7	8	9	10	11	
	American	7	8	9	10	11	12	
	Continental	39½	40½	41½	42½	43½	44½	
Men's shirts	British	14	14½	15	15½	16	16½	17	17½
	American	14	14½	15	15½	16	16½	17	17½
	Continental	36	37	38	39	40	41	42	43

▶ **Exercise 6**

You are buying various items in a branch of the department store Karstadt. Complete your part of the dialogue.

a You   *You would like to buy a scarf for your mother.*
Verkäuferin Welche Farbe?
b You   *Blue.*
Verkäuferin Dunkelblau oder hellblau?
c You   *Dark blue.*
Verkäuferin Dieser Schal hier ist sehr schön.
d You   *Is it wool?*
Verkäuferin Ja, natürlich. 100-prozentig.
e You   *How much does it cost?*
Verkäuferin €62,50.
f You   *That's a bit expensive.*
                  Ask if they have anything cheaper.
Verkäuferin Der karierte Schal kostet €28.
g You   *You'll take it.*

Now you want a pair of gloves for your friend.

h	**You**	*Say you'd like a pair of gloves.*
	Verkäuferin	Was für Handschuhe?
i	**You**	*Black, leather.*
	Verkäuferin	Welche Größe?
j	**You**	*You don't know.*
	Verkäuferin	Groß oder mittelgroß?
k	**You**	*Big.*
	Verkäuferin	Die kosten €43,50.
l	**You**	*Say you'll take them. And ask her to gift-wrap them.*

*Now you want a road map (**eine Straßenkarte**).*

m	**You**	*Have you got a road map?*
	Verkäuferin	In der Buchabteilung.
n	**You**	*Where is the book section?*
	Verkäuferin	Im vierten Stock.
o	**You**	*Ask where the lift is.*
	Verkäuferin	Dort drüben.
p	**You**	*Say thank you.*

▶ **Listening exercise 22**

What are these six customers buying?

Language notes

Here are some more useful phrases to do with shopping:

Ich kaufe ...	*I am buying*
Ich kaufe ein ...	*I am shopping*
Ich gehe einkaufen.	*I do the shopping.*
Ich habe gekauft	*I have bought*
Ich habe einen Mantel gekauft.	*I have bought a coat.*

Notice the word order in the last example. *I have a coat bought.*

ℹ Shops in Germany currently close at 6.30pm on weekdays and 2.00pm on Saturdays. However, it is likely that shops will soon be able to extend the opening hours to 8.00pm on weekdays and 4.00pm on Saturdays, although each region (**Land**) will retain the power to change Saturday closure by two hours either way.

Exercise 7

Look at the floor plan below. On which floor would you find...?

a leather goods
b books
c trainers
d records
e men's clothing
f children's clothing

g car parts
h tennis rackets
i model aircraft
j toilets
k confectionery
l ladies' clothing

```
Untergeschoss

Autozubehör
Werken und Bastein
Lebensmittel
```

```
2. Obergeschoss

Restaurant/Café
Reisebüro
WC
```

```
Erdgeschoss

Lederwaren
Schreibwaren
Tabakwaren
Bonbons
Kosmetik
Schmuck
Herrenbekleidung
```

```
3. Obergeschoss

Sportartikel
Sportkleidung
Schwimmsport
Sportschuhe
```

```
4. Obergeschoss

Buchhandlung
Musikgeschäft
Elektrogeschäft
Hauswaren
```

```
1. Obergeschoss

Kinder- und Damenbekleidung
```

Schmuck	*jewellery*
Autozubehör	*car accessories*
Werken und Basteln	*hobby and crafts*
die Rolltreppe	*escalator*
der Fahrstuhl/der Aufzug	*lift*

14

wann fährt der Zug?

when does the train leave?

In this unit you will learn how to
- use public transport in Germany
- ask for travel information
- buy tickets
- read the signs at the station
- work out what names mean

Am Bahnhof *At the station*

der Zug	*train*
mit dem Zug	*by train*
der Bus	*bus*
mit dem Bus	*by bus*
wann?	*when?*
das Gleis	*platform*
fahren	*to go*
ab/fahren	*to depart*
kommen	*to come*
an/kommen	*to arrive*
um	*at*
ab	*from*
Wann fährt der Zug ab?	*When does the train leave?*
Um wie viel Uhr fährt der Zug?	*At what time does the train leave?*
Wann kommt er in München an?	*When does it arrive in Munich? (lit: when comes he in Munich in?)*
Wo fährt der Zug nach München ab?	*Where does the Munich train leave from?*
Wann kommt der Bus aus London an?	*When does the bus from London arrive?*

Word patterns in questions

Look at the word order in the questions:

Wann **fährt** der Zug?	lit: *When **goes** the train?*
Wie **schreibt** man das?	*How **write** you that?*
Wie **geht** es Ihnen?	*How **goes** it to you?*
Wo **wohnen** Sie?	*Where **live** you?*

Language note

Nach usually means *after* as in **Nachmittag** *afternoon*, but it means *to* in expressions like **nach München, nach Italien.**

Exercise 1

Put the words in each of these sentences in the right order.

a der Zug in München wann kommt an?
b ab der Zug wann fährt?
c man schreibt wie das?
d wie es Ihnen geht?
e Sie wohnen wo?

Exercise 2

How would you say ...?

a to Munich
b to Italy

c from England
d from London

▶ Dialogue 27

Sie	Bahnbeamter
Wann fährt der Zug nach Hamburg?	
	Der nächste Zug nach Hamburg fährt um 11 Uhr 10.
Wann kommt er in Hamburg an?	
	Um 14 Uhr 46.
Wo fährt er ab?	
	Ab Gleis 7.
Und der nächste Zug nach Köln?	
	Der fährt um 11 Uhr 39.
Wann kommt er in Köln an?	
	Um 16 Uhr 27.
Wo fährt er ab?	
	Ab Gleis 14.

Abfahrt

Ankunft

Pronunciation tips

ab sounds ap
nächste [next-uh]

fährt [fair-t]
Köln [curl-n]

Learning notes

- Read the dialogue on page 137 and check that you can understand everything.
- Practise reading it out loud.
- Cover up the left-hand side. Remember, you want information about the trains to Hamburg and Köln. What questions are you going to ask?
- Now cover up the right-hand side. Here is the information that you need to make a different dialogue. See if you can do it. The train to Hamburg leaves at 12.15 from platform 8 and gets in at 15.13. The train to Köln leaves at 14.05 from platform 2 and gets in at 17.44.

i Before using public transport, buy a ticket from a machine (**Fahrausweise**). On boarding, you must get your ticket stamped in a ticket-cancelling machine (**Entwerter**) – often found at the top or bottom of the steps as you enter the vehicle.

Einmal nach Köln, bitte *A ticket to Cologne, please*

Sondertarife	*special fares*
die Fahrkarte	*ticket*
der Fahrplan	*timetable*
die Auskunft	*information*
die Abfahrt	*departure(s)*
die Ankunft	*arrival(s)*
der Bahnsteig	*platform*
das Gleis	*track, platform*
der Fahrkartenschalter	*ticket office*
der Fahrscheinautomat	*automatic ticket machine*
Schließfächer	*(left luggage) lockers*
das Gepäck	*luggage*
der Koffer	*suitcase*
der Kofferkuli	*luggage trolley*
der Speisewagen	*dining car*

der Schlafwagen	*sleeping car*
erste/zweite Klasse	*first/second class*
Raucher/Nichtraucher	*smoker/non-smoker*
Ich möchte ...	*I would like ...*
Ich möchte einen Platz reservieren.	*I would like to reserve a seat.*
Ich möchte eine Rückfahrkarte.	*I would like a return ticket.*
Ich möchte einmal einfach nach Hamburg.	*I would like a single to Hamburg.*
Ich möchte zweimal nach Bonn, hin und zurück.	*I would like 2 returns to Bonn.*
Ich möchte zweieinhalb.	*I would like two-and-a-half, i.e. 2 adults, 1 child.*
Ich möchte anderthalb.	*I would like one-and-a-half, i.e. 1 adult, 1 child.*
einsteigen	*to get on*
umsteigen	*to change*
aussteigen	*to get off*
Ich steige in Hamburg ein.	*I get on in Hamburg.*
Ich steige in Köln um.	*I change in Cologne.*
Ich steige in Stuttgart aus.	*I get off at Stuttgart.*
Was kostet es?	*How much is it?*
Ist dies der Zug nach Trier?	*Is this the train for Trier?*
Hat der Zug nach Dortmund Verspätung?	*Is the Dortmund train late?*
Muss ich umsteigen?	*Do I have to change?*
Wo muss ich umsteigen?	*Where do I have to change?*

Exercise 3

How would you ask for:

a   1 single to Berlin?

b   1 return to Salzburg?

c   3 returns to Mannheim?

d   2 returns to Koblenz?

e   2 singles to Osnabrück?

f   1 return to Innsbruck?

i A **Zuschlag** *supplement* is payable on all ICE trains and D trains for a journey under 50km.

Zuschlagpflichtig means you have to pay a supplement.

You usually have to put your ticket into an **Entwerter** to get the date stamped on it before getting on the train.

Abkürzungen *Abbreviations*

DB	Deutsche Bahn	*German railways*
ICE	InterCity Express	*Intercity express*
D	Express	*express*
E	Eilzug	*fast train*
N	Nahverkehr/Personenzug	*local train*
U-Bahn	Untergrundbahn	*underground (railway)*
S-Bahn	Schnell- oder Stadtbahn	*suburban railway*

▶ **Exercise 4**

Complete the dialogues following the guidelines given, and then practise them.

a　*You want a return ticket to Köln.*

Bahnbeamtin　Erste oder zweite Klasse?

b　**You**　*Second. Ask how much it is.*

Bahnbeamtin　€32.

c　**You**　*Ask when the train goes.*

Bahnbeamtin　Um halb elf.

d　**You**　*Ask where it goes from.*

Bahnbeamtin　Gleis 8.

e　**You**　*Say thank you.*

On your return journey ...

f　**You**　*Ask when the next train leaves for München.*

Bahnbeamtin　Es gibt einen InterCity um 10.53 Uhr und einen D-Zug um 11.18 Uhr.

g　**You**　*Ask how much it costs.*

Bahnbeamtin　Mit dem InterCity €63 und mit dem D-Zug €42.

h　**You**　*D-Zug! Do you have to change?*

Bahnbeamtin　Ja, in Koblenz.

i　**You**　*When do you get to München?*

Bahnbeamtin　Um 16.44 Uhr.

j　**You**　*Where does the train leave from?*

Bahnbeamtin　Ab Gleis 3.

▶ Listening exercise 23

Listen to the three customers, and for each, answer the following questions:

a Where are they going?
b What sort of ticket do they buy?
c When does the train leave?
d When does it get in?
e Do they have to change?
f How much does it cost?
g Which platform are they going from?

While staying in Germany you are going to ring the station to find out details about trains. Prepare a list of questions you are going to ask in each of these two situations:

a You are going on a business trip to Hamburg with a colleague.
b Going to Rüdesheim for the day with your friend.

Am Flughafen *At the airport*

das Flugzeug	*aeroplane*
der Flughafen	*airport*
der Flug	*flight*
die Flugnummer	*flight number*
der Flugsteig	*gate*
die Abflughalle	*departure lounge*
fliegen	*to fly*
die Maschine	*plane*
der Meldeschluss	*latest checking-in time*
der Fensterplatz	*window seat*
Wie lautet die Flugnummer?	*What's the flight number?*
Wann ist Meldeschluss?	*What is the latest checking-in time?*
Wann startet die Maschine?	*When does the plane take off?*
Wann landet die Maschine?	*When does the plane land?*
Was für eine Maschine ist es?	*What type of plane is it?*
Wie war die Reise?	*How was the journey?*
Ich bin müde	*I am tired*
Ich bin hungrig	*I am hungry*
Ich bin durstig	*I am thirsty*
Ich bin schläfrig	*I am sleepy*
Es geht mir gut	*I am fine*

Exercise 5

You are going to Germany. Prepare what you would tell your German friend on the phone. These are your flight details:

dep: Manchester   11.15
arr: London Heathrow   12.00
dep: London Heathrow   13.45
arr: Hamburg Fuhlsbüttel   14.15 (local time)
Flight number BA 5377

Exercise 6

You have rung up to find details of your return flight. How do you ask:

a When do you leave Hamburg?
b Is it a direct flight?
c What is your flight number?
d When are you due in Manchester?

Exercise 7

Complete your part in these telephone conversations with Fräulein Dellmann and Monika.

a	**You**	*Hallo. How are you?*
Frl. Dellmann		Gut danke und dir?
b	**You**	*You are fine too.*
Frl. Dellmann		Wann kommst du nach Düsseldorf?
c	**You**	*Sunday 26 October.*
Frl. Dellmann		Wann kommst du in Düsseldorf an?
d	**You**	*16.00.*
Frl. Dellmann		Wie lautet die Flugnummer?
e	**You**	*LH 123. Ask where you will meet.*
Frl. Dellmann		Ich hole dich vom Flughafen ab. (*I'll fetch you from the airport.*)
f	**You**	*Say you are looking forward to it.*
Frl. Dellmann		Bis dann. Tschüss!
g	**You**	*Tschüss! Bye!*
h	**You**	*Hallo. How are you?*
Monika		Gut danke, und dir?
i	**You**	*You are fine too. Ask when she is coming.*
Monika		Dienstag den 4.
j	**You**	*Ask at what time she is due in.*
Monika		Um 18.45 Uhr.

k	**You**	*Ask what the flight number is.*
	Monika	BA 345.
l	**You**	*Say you will meet her at the airport.*
	Monika	Gut. Ich freue mich schon darauf.
m	**You**	*Say till then, goodbye.*
	Monika	Auf Wiederhören.

Exercise 8

How would you say you are arriving at:

a 14.30 in Düsseldorf   d 18.35 in Hamburg
b 9.05 in Munich/München   e 21.20 in Vienna/Wien
c 11.30 in Cologne/Köln   f 17.45 in Frankfurt

▶ Listening exercise 24

When are these six travellers arriving and what are their flight numbers?

Language notes: What's in a name?

Many German placenames give you a clue about the whereabouts or origin of the place by including a word you already know. Here are a few examples:

die Brücke *the bridge*	**Innsbruck** bridge over the river Inn
	Saarbrücken bridges over the river Saar
die Burg *the castle*	**Freiburg, Hamburg, Augsburg ...** etc.
-chen *little*	**München** *little monks* München was originally a small settlement of monks
der Berg *mountain*	**Nürnberg** Nürn mountain, **Königsberg** King's mountain
das Dorf *village*	**Düsseldorf** village on the river Düssel
die Stadt *the town*	**Friedrichstadt** Frederick's town
der Mund *mouth*	**Dortmund** mouth of the river Dort
new *new*	**Neustadt** new town
der Bach *stream*	**Marbach** the Marbrook
der Wald *wood*	**Mittenwald** in the middle of the wood
das Tal *valley*	**Wuppertal** valley of the river Wupper
Baden *baths* (spa)	**Wiesbaden** spa on the Wiese (meadow)
der Hafen *harbour*	**Bremerhaven** port of Bremen
die Kirche *church*	**Oberkirch** upperchurch
das Heim *home*	**Rüdesheim** Rudi's home

der See *lake*   **Bodensee** (Lake Constance)
das Feld *field*   **Bielefeld**

Exercise 9

What do you think these names mean?

a	Wolfsburg	i	Neunkirchen	q	Steinbach
b	Fischbach	j	Friedrichshafen	r	Magdeburg
c	Neuburg	k	Zweibrücken	s	Osnabrück
d	Bad Ischl	l	Salzburg	t	der Schwarzwald
e	Gelsenkirchen	m	Chiemsee	u	Neustadt
f	Ingolstadt	n	Baden Baden	v	Rheinburg
g	Ammersee	o	Oberstdorf	w	Guntersdorf
h	Heidelberg	p	Mühlsdorf	x	Mannheim

i Names which we spell (or say) differently:

München *Munich,* **Wien** *Vienna,* **Köln** *Cologne,* **der Rhein** *Rhine (river),* **die Mosel** *Moselle (river),* **Braunschweig** *Brunswick,* **Hannover** *Hanover,* **Hameln** *Hamelin.*

15

essen und trinken

eating and drinking

In this unit you will learn how to
- recognize meal times
- ask for breakfast in a hotel
- ask for room service
- buy a snack
- call the waiter/waitress
- say you need something
- buy ice-creams and drinks

Zimmerservice *Room service*

das Frühstück	*breakfast*
das Mittagessen	*lunch*
das Abendessen	*evening meal*
ein/en Imbiss	*a snack*
Kaffee und Kuchen	*coffee and cakes*
die Sahne	*cream/evaporated milk*
die Milch	*milk*
Ei(er) (gekocht)	*egg(s) (boiled)*
Rührei	*scrambled egg*
Spiegelei(er)	*fried egg(s)*
das Brot/Brötchen	*bread/roll(s)*
Joghurt, Cornflakes und Müsli	*yoghurt, cornflakes and muesli*
Was essen Sie zum Frühstück?	*What do you eat for breakfast?*

der Schinken	*ham*	**der Speck**	*bacon*
die Wurst	*sausage*	**der Käse**	*cheese*
die Butter	*butter*	**der Zucker**	*sugar*
die Konfitüre	*jam*	**der Honig**	*honey*
der Toast	*toast*	**der Saft**	*juice*

Exercise 1

At what time ...

a can you have breakfast?
b is lunch served?
c can you get an evening meal?
d can you get a cup of coffee?

MAHLZEITEN	
FRÜHSTÜCKSBÜFFET	6.00–9.30
MITTAGESSEN	12.00–14.00
ABENDESSEN	18.00–22.00
KAFFEE IN DER KAFFEESTUBE	10.00–18.00

▶ Dialogue 28

Sie	der Kellner
	Guten Morgen. Tee oder Kaffee?
Kaffee, bitte.	
	Fruchtsaft oder Cornflakes?
Orangensaft.	

Essen Sie ein Ei?

Nein, danke.

Toast oder Brötchen?

Brötchen.
Haben Sie noch Milch?

Bitte schön.

You would like to take breakfast in your room. Fill out the breakfast order.

TRUSTEE • Park Hotel • München

Guten Morgen!

Zimmer-Frühstücksbestellung

Zimmer Nr.	Gast	Personenzahl

Frühstück
Wann möchten Sie Ihr Frühstück – bitte kreuzen Sie die gewünschte Uhrzeit an:

☐ 7.00 Uhr ☐ 7.30 Uhr ☐ 8.00 Uhr

☐ 8.30 Uhr ☐ 9.00 Uhr ☐ 9.30 Uhr

☐ 10.00 Uhr ☐ 10.30 Uhr

Bitte hängen Sie die ausgefüllte Frühstückskarte bereits am Abend an den Türknopf.

"Trustee Frühstück" €20

☐ Kaffee ☐ Tee mit Zitrone ☐ Schokolade

☐ Orangensaft ☐ Tee mit Sahne ☐ Milch kalt

☐ Grapefruitsaft ☐ Ei gekocht ☐ Milch heiß

☐ Schinken ☐ Wurst ☐ Käse

☐ Brot (Schwarzbrot/Weißbrot), Brötchen, Croissant, Butter, Konfitüre, Honig

---

Auf Ihren Wunsch

☐ 2 Spiegeleier ☐ 2 Rühreier €3,20

☐ Mit Schinken ☐ Mit Speck €3,90

Unterschrift Total

Die Preise enthalten Service und gesetzliche Mehrwertsteuer.
Etagenaufschlag €3,50

| der Türknopf | door knob |
| auf Ihren Wunsch | at your request (extras) |

Learning note

• Practise the dialogue, ordering different things.

Ich möchte einen Imbiss *I'd like a snack*

eine Portion	a portion
Bratwurst	grilled sausage
Bockwurst	boiled sausage (Frankfurter type)
die Pommes (frites)	chips
der Senf	mustard
mit Ketchup	ketchup
die Mayonnaise (now also written as Majonäse)	mayonnaise
Reibekuchen mit Apfelmus	thin potato fritters with apple purée
Waffeln mit Kirschsoße	waffles with cherry sauce
eine Dose Cola	a can of coca cola
ein Glas Limo	a glass of lemonade
eine Flasche Sprudel	a bottle of carbonated water
Wasser	water
einen Apfelsaft	apple juice
Apfelschorle (Apfelsaft mit Limo)	apple juice with lemonade
ein Bier	beer
ein Glas Wein	a glass of wine
Kleingeld	(small) change
und	and
Bitte schön.	Here you are.
zurück	change (lit: back)
Einmal Bratwurst mit Kartoffelsalat.	Sausage and potato salad for one.
Zweimal Currywurst mit Püree.	Curried sausage with potato purée for two.

Exercise 2

How would you order these?

a chips; **b** 2 grilled sausages; **c** sausage (frankfurter) and chips × 2; **d** can of coke; **e** a beer; **f** 2 waffles

▶ Listening exercise 25

What have these eight customers ordered?

▶ Exercise 3

Ich möchte ...

Complete your part of the dialogue.

a	**You**	*You would like a sausage and chips.*
	Kellner	Ketchup oder Mayo?
b	**You**	*Ketchup.*
	Kellner	Bitte schön. Sonst noch etwas?
c	**You**	*Your friend wants a curry sausage and potato salad.*
	Kellner	Bitte schön. Und zu trinken?
d	**You**	*You want a coke and your friend wants a beer. That's all. Ask how much it is.*
	Kellner	Das macht €22.
e	**You**	*Here you are: €50.*
	Kellner	Haben Sie Kleingeld?
f	**You**	*I have €2.*
	Kellner	So, €30 zurück.

Exercise 4

Where would you expect to get the following meals or snacks? Match each one with a place.

a a quick snack; **b** coffee and cakes; **c** a pizza; **d** a self-service meal; **e** a meal and a drink (more than one place); **f** an ice-cream

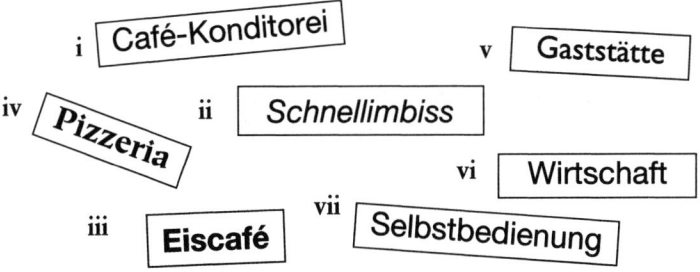

i Café-Konditorei

v Gaststätte

iv Pizzeria

ii Schnellimbiss

vi Wirtschaft

iii Eiscafé

vii Selbstbedienung

Learning note

* Choose a snack for yourself and two friends and work out what you would have to say to order it.

An dem Tisch *At the table*

der Suppenteller	*soup bowl*		
der Becher (–)	*beaker/mug*		
noch	*more* (lit: still)/*another*		
die Soße	*sauce*		
der Teller (–)	*plate*	**die Tasse (n)**	*cup*
die Untertasse (n)	*saucer*	**die Schüssel (n)**	*bowl*
das Messer (–)	*knife*	**das Glas (¨er)**	*glass*
das Salz	*salt*	**der Pfeffer**	*pepper*
die Gabel (n)	*fork*	**der Löffel (–)**	*spoon*

Word patterns

Ich habe	**keinen Teller**	masculine	(**der** words)
	keine Tasse	feminine	(**die** words)
	kein Messer	neuter	(**das** words)

Ich brauche	**einen Teller**	(**der**)
	eine Tasse	(**die**)
	ein Messer	(**das**)

You won't be prevented from communicating effectively if you don't know whether a word is **der, die** or **das** because you can convey the meaning perfectly well without the ending. German speakers do not always pronounce them clearly themselves.

i To get the waiter's/waitress's attention, you can use:

Fräulein!	*Miss!* (calling the waitress – whatever her age)
Herr Ober!	*Waiter!* (rather formal)

Or less formally

Bitte!   *Please!*

The standard reply is:

(Ich) komme gleich.   *(I'll) be right with you.*

Soße as a word on its own usually means custard, a sweet sauce or gravy.

Pudding is blancmange; it doesn't mean pudding in the sense of dessert.

Exercise 5

a How would you ask for:

b And how would you ask for more:

Exercise 6

Complete your part of the dialogues.

a	**You**	*Attract the waiter's attention.*
	Kellner	Ja?
b	**You**	*You need another plate ...*
	Kellner	Bitte schön.
c	**You**	*And the salt pot is empty ...*
	Kellner	Bitte schön.

d You	*And have they got any ketchup?*
Kellner	Sonst noch etwas?
e You	*No, thanks that's all!*
f You	*Try to attract her attention.*
Kellner	Ja, bitte schön.
g You	*You need another glass.*
Kellner	Bitte schön.
h You	*Have they got any OK Sauce?*
Kellner	Es tut mir Leid.
i You	*You would like another beer and a glass of lemonade.*

Word building

Here are a few more examples of how German words are often combinations of two words:

der Löffel *spoon*	**Ess-** *eating/dining*
Ess<u>löffel</u>	<u>Ess</u>zimmer
Tee<u>löffel</u>	<u>Ess</u>ecke
Kaffee<u>löffel</u>	<u>Ess</u>bar
Koch<u>löffel</u>	<u>Ess</u>tisch

Exercise 7

Taschen- *pocket*   **Küchen-** *kitchen*   **Brot-** *bread*

How would you say:

a pocket knife?   **b** kitchen knife?   **c** bread knife?

In der Eisdiele *At the ice-cream parlour*

▶ Dialogue 29

Sie	die Kellnerin
	Was darf es sein?
Ich möchte ein Eis.	
	Hier ist die Eiskarte.
Ich möchte einmal Pfirsich Melba und einmal Bananen-Split.	
	Mit Sahne?

Ja, mit Sahne.

Ja. Lecker!

Hat es geschmeckt?

DIE EISKARTE

Venediger — Walnuss- und Pistazieneiscreme mit Nüssen und Schlagsahne

Kopenhagener — Vanilleeis mit warmer Schokosoße und Schlagsahne

Schwarzwälder — Schoko- und Vanilleeis mit Kirschwasser und Sauerkirschen und Schlagsahne

Florentiner — Schoko-, Nuss- und Vanilleeis mit Schlagsahne

Kalifornien — Pfirsich-Eiscreme mit Pfirsichstücken, Himbeersoße und Schlagsahne

Wiener — Mokka- und Vanilleneiscreme mit Baiserstückchen, Schlagsahne und Schokosoße

Italiener — Spaghettieis mit Erdbeersoße und Kokosflocken

---

die Schlagsahne	*whipped cream*
das Schlagobers	*whipped cream* (S. Germany and Austria)
Mokka-	*coffee*
das Baiser/die Meringe	*meringue*
die Kokosflocken	*coconut flakes*
der Streusel	*hundreds and thousands*
Welchen Geschmack?	*Which flavour?*
Hat es geschmeckt?	*Did you like it?* (lit: Has it tasted (good)?)
das Walnusseis	*walnut ice-cream*
das Vanilleeis	*vanilla ice-cream*
das Zitroneneis	*lemon ice-cream*
das Milcheis	*milk ice-cream*
das Fruchteis	*fruit sorbet*

Learning notes

- Choose an ice-cream for yourself and your friend.
- Make up an ice-cream!

Was kostet das? *What does it cost?*

Biere		Weine (1/4 l Karaffe)	
Löwenbräu	€3,70	Mosel (Bernkastel)	€5,90
Export dunkel	€3,60	Rhein (Liebfraumilch)	€5,90
Export hell	€3,60	Beaujolais	€6,50
Alkoholfreies Bier	€3,60	Tafelwein	€4,80
Warme Getränke		**Kalte Getränke**	
Tasse Kaffee	€2,50	Fanta	€2,50
Tasse Kaffee koffeinfrei	€2,50	Cola	€2,60
Kännchen Kaffee	€4,80	Tonic Water	€2,60
Glas Tee		Mineralwasser	€2,50
(mit Zitrone oder Milch)	€2,60		
Kännchen Tee	€4,80	Orangensaft	€3,30
Glas Tee mit Rum	€6,10	Apfelsaft	€2,50
Tasse Schokolade	€2,40	Limo	€2,30
Kännchen Schokolade	€4,80	Radler/Alterwasser	
		(North Germany)	€3,00

Exercise 8

Was kostet das?

16 im Restaurant
in the restaurant

In this unit you will learn how to

- understand a menu
- recognize the names of various dishes
- say what you like and don't like
- ask for recommendations
- say you are vegetarian

Ist hier noch frei? *Is anyone sitting here?*

die Speisekarte	*menu*
die Weinliste	*wine list*
das Tagesgericht	*dish of the day*
die Tagessuppe	*soup of the day*
die Fleischgerichte	*meat dishes*
die Fischgerichte	*fish dishes*
die Vorspeisen	*hors d'oeuvres*
das Hauptgericht	*main course*
das Gemüse	*vegetables*
der Nachtisch	*dessert*
die Getränke	*drinks*
frisch gemacht	*freshly made*
hausgemacht	*home-made*
Was können Sie empfehlen?	*What can you recommend?*
Ich bin Vegetarier/in.	*I am a vegetarian.*
Ich esse kein Fleisch.	*I don't eat meat.*
Mir schmeckt es nicht.	*I don't like (the taste of) it.*
Es schmeckt mir gut.	*I like (the taste of) it.*
Schmeckt's?	*Do you like it?*
Hat es geschmeckt?	*Did you like it?*
Ja, es schmeckt sehr gut.	*Yes, it is very nice.*
lecker	*delicious*
Es ist zu sauer	*It is too sour*
Es ist zu scharf	*It is too hot (sharp)*
Es ist zu süß	*It is too sweet*

Learning notes

- See if you can pair these up without looking at the **Key words**:

die Speisekarte	soup of the day
die Weinliste	dish of the day
das Tagesgericht	dessert
die Tagessuppe	main course
die Fleischgerichte	the menu
die Fischgerichte	the wine list
die Vorspeisen	meat dishes
das Hauptgericht	drinks
das Gemüse	fish dishes
der Nachtisch	hors d'oeuvres
die Getränke	vegetables

- Now cover up the German and see if you can remember it.

▶ Dialogue 30

Sie	der Kellner
Ist hier noch frei bitte?	
	Der Tisch in der Ecke ist frei.
Die Speisekarte bitte.	
	Bitte schön.
Was können Sie empfehlen?	
	Die Leberklöße sind frisch gemacht.
Das schmeckt mir nicht.	
	Wie wäre es mit dem Schweinefilet mit Champignonrahmsauce und hausgemachten Nudeln?
Gut. Ich nehme es. Mein Freund ist Vegetarier.	
	Wie wäre es mit einer hausgemachten Gemüselasagne?
Gut. Wir nehmen einmal Tagessuppe und einmal Aufschnittplatte als Vorspeise.	
	Und als Nachtisch?
Einmal Rote Grütze.	
	Mit Sahne, Milch oder Vanillesosse?
Mit Vanillesosse und einmal Apfelstrudel.	
	Was trinken Sie?
Ein Glas Hauswein.	
	Rot oder weiß?
Rot, und ein Glas Sprudel.	
	Mit Geschmack?
Nein, ohne.	

Leberklöße	*liver dumplings*
die Champignonrahmsauce	*cream of mushroom sauce*
Nudeln	*pasta/noodles*
Gemüselasagne	*vegeable lasagne*
Aufschnittplatte	*cold sliced meats (ham and salami)*
die Rote Grütze	*a compote of red fruit (redcurrants, raspberries, etc.)*
der Hauswein	*house wine*
mit Geschmack	*flavoured (lemonade/ orangeade etc.)*

Learning notes

- Read the dialogue and check that you understand everything.
- Read it out loud.

Die Speisekarte *The menu*

Fleischgerichte	*meat dishes*
das Rindfleisch	*beef*
das Schweinefleisch	*pork*
das Hammelfleisch	*mutton*
das Hackfleisch	*mincemeat*
der Schaschlik	*kebab*
das Lammfleisch	*lamb*
Fischgerichte	*fish dishes*
das Fischfilet	*fish fillet*
der Kabeljau	*cod*
die Forelle	*trout*
der Lachs	*salmon*
der Hering	*herring*
der Matjes	*pickled herring*
Krabben	*shrimps/prawns*
das Geflügel	*poultry*
das Hähnchen	*chicken*
der Truthahn	*turkey*
die Gans	*goose*
die Ente	*duck*

das Omelett	omelette
das Gemüse	vegetables
Kartoffeln	potatoes
Folienkartoffeln	baked potatoes (cooked in foil)
Salzkartoffeln	boiled potatoes (lit: salt potatoes)
Bratkartoffeln	fried potatoes
Pommes (frites)	chips
Erbsen	peas
Bohnen	beans
Karotten	carrots
der Spinat	spinach
der Spargel	asparagus
Bambussprossen	bamboo shoots
der Blumenkohl	cauliflower
der Kohl	cabbage
der Weißkohl	white cabbage
der Rotkohl	red cabbage
das Sauerkraut	sour pickled cabbage
der Salat	lettuce

Wienerschnitzel (Viennese Schnitzel) is a thin slice of veal or pork, which is dipped in egg before being covered with breadcrumbs and lightly fried.

Jägerschnitzel (hunter's Schnitzel) is the same meat not covered in breadcrumbs, fried lightly and served with a tomato and mushroom sauce.

Zigeunerschnitzel (gypsy's Schnitzel) is the same meat again without breadcrumbs, fried lightly and served with a piquant sauce with spices and green pepper.

▶ Dialogue 31

Sie	der Kellner
Entschuldigung. Ist hier noch frei?	
	Ja, bitte schön. Hier ist die Speisekarte.
Was für eine Tagessuppe gibt es heute?	
	Champignonrahmsuppe.

Also, einmal Tagessuppe für
mich und einmal Melone
mit Parmaschinken.

Und als Hauptgericht?

Ich möchte einmal
Wienerschnitzel mit
Pommes und grünem Salat
und einmal
Schweineroulade mit
Butternudeln.

Was trinken Sie?

Ein Glas Rotwein und ein
Glas Sprudel.

Und als Nachtisch?

Haben Sie Obstsalat?

Nein, leider nicht.
Aber der Apfelstrudel ist
gut.

Was ist das?

Apfel, Rosinen und Zimt in
Blätterteig mit Vanillesosse.

Das sieht gut aus.
Einmal Apfelstrudel und
einmal Erdbeertorte.

Mit Sahne?

Nein danke, ohne Sahne.

Learning tips

- Read the dialogue carefully and make sure you understand
  everything. There are a few words that you have not met
  before. Can you work out what they mean?
- Read it out loud. Cover the left-hand side and answer the
  questions for yourself and a friend.
- Cover up the right-hand side and see if you can remember
  what the questions were.

▶ Listening exercise 26

What do these six customers order?

Gern und lieber *Liking and preferring*

Essen Sie gern ...?/Isst du gern ...?	*Do you like (to eat ...)?*
Trinken Sie gern ...?	*Do you like (to drink ...)?*
Ich esse gern ...	*I like (to eat ...)*
Ich esse lieber ...	*I prefer (I would rather eat ...)*
Ich trinke gern ...	*I like (to drink ...)*
Ich trinke lieber	*I prefer (I would rather drink ...)*
Ich mag ...	*I like ...*
Ich mag keine Pommes.	*I don't like chips.* (lit: I like no ...)
Trinken Sie gern ein Glas Wein?	*Would you like a glass of wine?*

Word patterns

Here are two different ways of saying you like something:

Using *gern* ('willingly')

When you use **gern** you have to say what it is that you like doing.

Ich	esse trinke spiele tanze	gern	**Gehen** Sie gern ins Restaurant? **Essen** Sie gern Chinesisch? **Trinken** Sie gern Bier?

Using *ich mag* ('I like')

This seems easier to use because it is more like the English:

Ich mag Bier.	*I like beer.*
but ...	
Ich mag Bier sehr gern.	*I like beer very much.*
Ich mag kein Bier.	*I don't like beer.*
And you prefer ...	
Ich mag Tee, aber ich trinke lieber Kaffee.	*I like tea but I prefer (to drink) coffee.*
Ich trinke gern schwarzen Tee, aber ich trinke lieber Früchtetee.	*I like (to drink) tea but I prefer to drink) fruit/herbal tea.*

Exercise 1

You want to know if your friend likes these. How would you ask?

ℹ️ Ordinary tea is sometimes called 'black tea' to distinguish it from the many herbal teas that are drunk in Germany.

Exercise 2 Im Restaurant *In the resturant*

Complete your part of the dialogue, using the **Key words** on pages 158–9 or, if you prefer, the menu on pages 164–5.

a	**You**	*Ask if this place is free.*
	Kellner	Ja, bitte schön. Hier ist die Speisekarte.
b	**You**	*Find out what the soup of the day is today.*
	Kellner	Gemüsesuppe.
c	**You**	*Ask if they have tomato soup.*
	Kellner	Nein, heute nicht.
d	**You**	*Ask for something else.*
	Kellner	Und als Hauptgericht? Das Schnitzel ist gut.
e	**You**	*No, you don't like Schnitzel.*
	Kellner	Essen Sie gern Fisch?
f	**You**	*Choose what you would like from the menu.*
	Kellner	Und als Gemüse?
g	**You**	*Choose a suitable vegetable or salad.*
	Kellner	Was trinken Sie?
h	**You**	*Choose something to drink.*
	Kellner	Und als Nachtisch?
i	**You**	*Ask what they recommend.*
	Kellner	Erdbeertorte.

j **You**	*Say you'll take it.*
Kellner	Mit Sahne?
k **You**	*Say yes, with cream.*
Kellner	Trinken Sie einen Kaffee?
l **You**	*Say yes, please.*

Learning note

- Read the dialogue out loud and check that you understand all the German.

Zahlen, bitte *The bill, please*

Zahlen, bitte.	*Bill, please.* (lit: pay please)
Zusammen oder getrennt?	*Together or separate?*
mit Bedienung	*with service*
ohne Bedienung	*without service*
MWSt (Mehrwertsteuer)	*VAT*
Ich bin satt.	*I am full.*
Hat es geschmeckt?	*Did you like it?* (lit: has it tasted (good)?)
Das ist für Sie.	*That's for you.*
das Kleingeld	*change* (lit: small money)
das Trinkgeld	*tip* (lit: drink money)

▶ Dialogue 32

Sie	Kellnerin
Zahlen, bitte.	
	Hat es geschmeckt?
Ja, lecker.	
	Zusammen oder getrennt?
Zusammen.	
	Das macht €64,25.
Nehmen Sie Kreditkarten?	
	Nein. Leider nicht.
Ich habe nur eine 100 Euro Banknote.	
	Ich habe Kleingeld.
Das ist für Sie.	
	Vielen Dank. Auf Wiedersehen.

Learning notes

- Read the dialogue and check you understand everything.
- Practise your part of the dialogue out loud.

Exercise 3

These are questions you might be asked. What do they mean?

a Trinken Sie etwas dazu?
b Möchten Sie einen Nachtisch?
c Welchen Geschmack?
d Möchten Sie Ketchup?
e Hat es geschmeckt?
f Zusammen oder getrennt?

i The service charge is almost always included in the bill, but if you have been satisfied with the service it is normal to give an additional tip or to leave the small change, though anything under €0,60 might be considered insulting. If you want to take the food with you, you would order: 'Zum Mitnehmen, bitte'.

Kaffeetrinken Modern coffees for the 'Starbucks brigade' include **Espresso, doppelter Espresso, Milchkaffee, Kaffee HAG (ohne Koffein)** and **Kapuziner** or **Cappuccino**.

Kaffeespezialitäten

Cappuccino mit Milch oder Sahne	€3,30
Milchkaffee	€3,60
Latte Macchiato	€4,00
Kännchen Schoko-Kaffee: ½ Schoko, ½ Kaffee	€4,50
Espresso	€2,40

Espresso, doppelt	€4,10
Tasse Kaffee	€2,30
Kännchen Kaffee	€4,60
Tasse Mocca	€2,40
Kännchen Mocca	€4,60
Tasse Kaffee, entkoffeiniert	€2,30
Tasse Schokolade mit Sahne geschlagen	€4,60
Sirup: Caramel, Vanille, Amaretto, Haselnuss	€0,50

17

die Freizeit
free time

In this unit you will learn how to
- say what you like doing in your free time
- ask someone what they would like to do
- take part in sports and hobbies
- make arrangements
- go about summer and winter activities

Was machen Sie gern und	*What do you like and not like*
was machen Sie nicht gern?	*doing?*
in meiner Freizeit	*in my free time*
in Ihrer Freizeit	*in your free time*
Schwimmen Sie gern?	*Do you like swimming?*
Ich schwimme gern.	*I like swimming.*
Lesen Sie gern?	*Do you like reading?*
Ich lese gern.	*I like reading.*
Tanzen Sie gern?	*Do you like dancing?*
Ich tanze gern.	*I like dancing.*

Using *gehen* with a sport or pastime

Gehen Sie gern	wandern	*Do you like to go hiking?*
	spazieren?	*for walks?*
	schwimmen?	*swimming?*
	ins Kino?	*to the cinema?*
	in ein Nachtlokal?	*to a night club?*
	joggen?	*jogging?*

Using *spielen*

Spielen Sie gern	Tennis?	*Do you like playing tennis?*
	Karten?	*cards?*
	Snooker?	*snooker?*
	Schach?	*chess?*
	Squash?	*squash?*
	Fußball?	*football?*

Separable verbs

Ski laufen *to ski*	**Laufen** sie gern **Ski?**	Ich **laufe** gern **Ski.**
fernsehen *to watch TV*	**Sehen** Sie gern **fern?**	Ich **sehe** gern **fern.**
Rad fahren *to ride a bike*	**Fahren** Sie gern **Rad?**	Ich **fahre** gern **Rad.**

These are all verbs which split up and the prefix (first part of the word) goes to the end of the sentence.

Pronunciation tip

Ski sounds **shee**.

Exercise 1

What would you ask Fräulein Hoffmann to find out if she likes to:

a go to the cinema?
b go dancing?
c go swimming?

d play cards?
e go cycling?
f watch TV?

▶ Dialogue 33

Sie	Herr Schwarz
Was machen wir heute Abend?	
Spielen Sie gern Squash?	
	Ja, sehr gern.
Gut. Wir spielen Squash. Schwimmen Sie auch gern?	
	Ja. Ich schwimme gern.
Gut, wir spielen Squash und dann gehen wir schwimmen und danach gehen wir in ein Restaurant.	
	Gut. Ich freue mich schon darauf!
Was machen wir heute Abend?	
Spielen Sie gern Tennis?	
	Nein. Leider nicht. Mein Rücken tut weh.
Was machen Sie gern?	
	Ich gehe gern tanzen oder ins Kino.
Gut. Wir gehen zuerst ins Kino und danach in ein Nachtlokal.	

dann/danach	then
zuerst	first

Exercise 2

How would you ask Herr Schwarz's ten-year-old son if he likes to:

a	play squash?	c	ski?	e	ride a bike?
b	play football?	d	play tennis?	f	play chess?

Exercise 3

Was machen Sie gern in Ihrer Freizeit?
How would these people answer?

a b c d e f

▶ **Listening exercise 27**

What do these six people like and not like doing?

Haben Sie Lust mitzukommen? *Would you like to come too?*

mitkommen	*to come too (a splitting verb)*
	(lit: to come with (me/us/you))
Ich komme mit.	*I'll come too.*
vorbeikommen	*to come past*
Ich komme ... vorbei.	*I'm coming past ...*
abholen	*to fetch*
Ich hole ... ab.	*I'm fetching ...*
zurückkommen	*to come back*

Ich komme um ... zurück.	*I'm coming back at ...*
das Spiel	*game*
gegen	*against*
danach	*afterwards*
vor	*in front of*
Ich habe Lust Tennis zu spielen.	*I would like to play tennis.*
Haben Sie Lust Tennis zu spielen?/Möchten sie Tennis spielen?	*Would you like to play tennis?*
Nein, ich habe keine Lust ...	*No, I don't want to ...*
Ich gehe lieber ...	*I would rather ...*
angeln	*to fish*
Ich bin noch nicht Ski gefahren.	*I haven't skied before.*
Wo/Wann treffen wir uns?	*Where/When shall we meet?*
Ich freue mich schon darauf.	*I am looking forward to it.*
heute	*today*
heute früh/morgen, heute Vormittag	*morning*
heute Nachmittag	*afternoon*
heute Abend	*evening*
morgen	*tomorrow*
morgen früh, morgen Vormittag	*tomorrow morning*
morgen Nachmittag	*tomorrow afternoon*
morgen Abend	*tomorrow evening*

Exercise 4

Hannelore is staying with you. Tell her:

a   You are going to play tennis tomorrow morning. Would she like to come?

b   You are going swimming tomorrow evening. Would she like to come?

c   You are going to play cards this evening. Does she want to play?

d   You are going fishing this afternoon. Does she want to come?

e   You are going to a night club tonight. Is she going to come?

Jürgen is staying with you.

f   Tell him you are going to the local football match on Saturday afternoon.

g Ask him if he would like to come with you.
h Tell him when the match begins.
i Ask him if he would like to play tennis afterwards.

▶ Exercise 5

Complete your part of the dialogues with Hans-Peter.

Hans-Peter	Morgen Nachmittag gehen wir zum Fußball, Düsseldorf gegen Bayern-München. Haben Sie Lust mitzukommen?
a **You**	*Yes, you would like to. What time?*
Hans-Peter	Das Spiel beginnt um 14.30 Uhr.
	Wir treffen uns um 13.00 Uhr.
b **You**	*Ask where you should meet.*
Hans-Peter	Ich komme vorbei und hole Sie ab.
Hans-Peter	Morgen Nachmittag gehen wir zum Fußball, Düsseldorf gegen Bayern-München. Haben Sie Lust mitzukommen?
c **You**	*No, you don't want to.*
	You would rather play tennis.
Hans-Peter	Gut. Wir spielen danach Tennis.
d **You**	*Ask what time.*
Hans-Peter	Um sechs.
e **You**	*Find out where to meet.*
Hans-Peter	Vor der Tennishalle.
Hans-Peter	Wir fahren morgen Ski.
	Kommen Sie mit?
f **You**	*Yes, I'll come too but I have not skied before!*
Hans-Peter	Kein Problem!
	Jürgen ist Skilehrer.
g **You**	*Find out when you are going.*
Hans-Peter	Wir fahren um 7.30 Uhr ab.
h **You**	*And when you are due back?*
Hans-Peter	So, um halb zehn.
i **You**	*Good. You are looking forward to it.*
Hans-Peter	Bis dann, tschüss.

Im Sommer *In summer*

am Strand	*on the beach*
in den Bergen	*in the mountains*
auf dem Land	*in the country*
in der Stadt	*in the town*
an der Küste	*on the coast*
am Mittelmeer	*on the Mediterranean*
die Ferien	*holidays*
das Angebot	*offer*
Wo verbringen Sie Ihre Ferien?	*Where do you spend your holidays?*
Ich verbringe meine Ferien in den Bergen/an der Küste/ auf dem Bauernhof.	*I spend my holidays in the mountains/on the coast/ on the farm.*

Word patterns

An, in and **auf** are trigger words which sometimes (but not always) change **der, die** and **das**, as we've seen before.

masc.	**der** to **dem**
fem.	**die** to **der**
neut.	**das** to **dem**
plural	**die** to **den**

an + dem = am   **zu + dem = zum**
in + dem = im   **zu + der = zur**

Exercise 6

Can you say which 13 activities are being offered at Sonnenstrand?

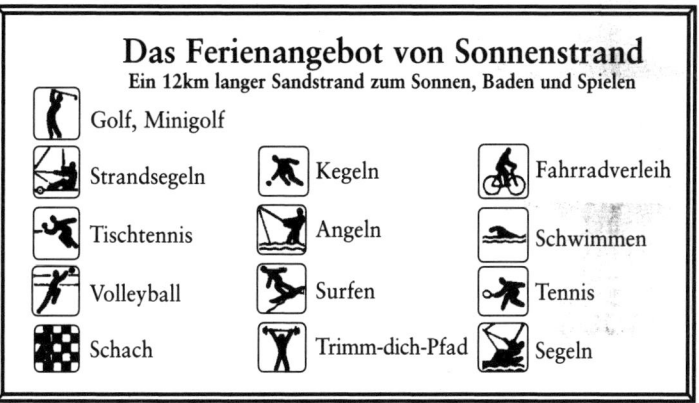

Das Ferienangebot von Sonnenstrand
Ein 12km langer Sandstrand zum Sonnen, Baden und Spielen

Golf, Minigolf

Strandsegeln   Kegeln   Fahrradverleih

Tischtennis   Angeln   Schwimmen

Volleyball   Surfen   Tennis

Schach   Trimm-dich-Pfad   Segeln

Kegeln	bowling
Strandsegeln	sand yachting
Fahrradverleih	bicycle hire
Trimm-dich-Pfad	a fitness circuit laid out usually in a park or woodland

▶ Dialogue 34: Ich sonne mich *I am sunbathing*

Sie	Hannelore
Wo verbringen Sie Ihre Ferien?	
	Im Winter verbringen wir unsere Ferien in den Alpen. Wir fahren gern Ski.
Und im Sommer?	
	An der Ostseeküste.
Was machen Sie dort?	
	Wenn das Wetter gut ist, gehen wir schwimmen und wir sonnen uns oder wir gehen surfen oder segeln.
Und wenn es schlecht ist?	
	Dann gehen wir ins Kino, oder wir machen einen Stadtbummel. Und Sie?
Wenn das Wetter schlecht ist, bleibe ich zu Hause, sehe fern oder lese ein Buch.	
	Wo verbringen Sie Ihre Ferien?
An der Küste oder in den Bergen.	
	Und was machen Sie?
Wir schwimmen und sonnen uns oder wir machen Wanderungen.	
	Was macht Herr Thomas?
Er spielt Golf oder geht angeln.	
	Und was machen die Kinder?
Peter spielt Tennis und fährt gern Rad und Mary verbringt den ganzen Tag am Strand.	

> **den ganzen Tag** *the whole day*
> **Ich bleibe zu Hause.** *I stay at home.*
> **der Stadtbummel** *stroll in town*

Exercise 7

Was machen Sie gern, **a** wenn das Wetter gut ist? **b** wenn das Wetter schlecht ist? (Tick the appropriate activities.)

i Ich sonne mich.

ii Ich sehe fern.

iii Ich lese ein Buch.

iv Ich spiele Tennis.

v Ich gehe schwimmen.

vi Ich spiele Karten.

vii Ich gehe surfen.

viii Ich gehe ins Kino.

ix Ich gehe joggen.

x Ich sehe fern.

▶ Listening exercise 28

Was machen sie? *What do they do?*

Im Winter *In winter*

> **die Möglichkeiten** *possibilities*
> **Pferdeschlittenfahrten** *horse-drawn sleigh rides*
> **der Schnee** *snow*
> **verschneit** *snow-covered*
> **der Weg (e)** *path*
> **durch den Wald** *through the wood*
> **die Piste** *piste*
> **schön** *nice*
> **geräumt** *cleared*
> **rodeln** *to sledge, toboggan*
> **die Rodelbahn** *sledge track, toboggan run*
> **Langlauf** *cross-country skiing*
> **die Loipe** *cross-country ski route*
> **Eislaufen** *skating (lit: ice running)*
> **am See** *on the lake*
> **oder** *or*
> **auf der Eislaufbahn** *on the ice-rink*
> **Eisstockschießen** *a game rather like curling*
> **die Gondelbahn** *cable railway*
> **der Sessellift** *chair lift*
> **der Schlepplift** *drag lift*

der Waldweg	*woodland path*
entspannen	*to relax*
Kegeln	*bowling*
die Kegelbahn	*bowling alley*

Word building

Use these vocabulary clues and words you already know to do Exercise 8:

der Schnee	*snow*
die Schlacht	*fight, battle*
die Flocke	*flake*
das Glöckchen	*little bell*
die Kette(n)	*chain(s)*
die Brille	*glasses*
die Raupe	*caterpillar*
der Sturm	*storm*
es schneit	*it is snowing*
verschneit	*snow-covered*

Exercise 8

How many of these new words can you make?

a	snowman	**d**	snowflake	**g**	snow goggles
b	snowball	**e**	snowdrop	**h**	snow-cat
c	snowball fight	**f**	snowchains	**i**	snow storm

18

Autofahren in Deutschland

motoring in Germany

In this unit you will learn how to
- buy petrol
- drive on German motorways
- use the emergency services
- cope in the event of breakdown or accident
- park

An der Tankstelle *At the petrol station*

die Tankstelle	*petrol station*
die Raststätte	*service area*
das Benzin	*petrol*
der Diesel	*diesel*
der/das Liter	*litre*
das Wasser	*water*
das Öl	*oil*
die Luft	*air*
volltanken	*to fill up*
prüfen	*to check*
der Reifen (-)	*tyre*
der Reifendruck	*tyre pressue*
Selbsttanken	*self-service petrol*
Münztank	*coin-operated pump*
Können Sie ...?	*Can you ...?*
Können Sie den Reifendruck prüfen?	*Can you check the tyres?*
Können Sie den Ölstand prüfen?	*Can you check the oil?*
Können Sie die Windschutzscheibe putzen?	*Can you clean the windscreen?*
Hier ist meine Kreditkarte.	*Here is my credit card.*

i Most garages are now self-service, but if you buy petrol at the motorway services you will occasionally be served and the attendant will sometimes also wash the windscreen and expect a small tip.

Learning notes
- Read all the words out loud.
- Cover up the English and see if you know what they all mean.
- Cover up the German and see if you can remember it.

▶ Listening exercise 29
What are these six customers asking?

 Dialogue 35

Sie	Tankwart
Guten Tag.	
	Guten Tag.
Volltanken, bitte.	
	Benzin oder Diesel?
Diesel.	
	So, bitte schön.
Wo muss ich zahlen?	
	An der Kasse, dort drüben.
Danke schön.	

Auf der Autobahn *On the motorway*

die Autobahn	*motorway*
das Autobahndreieck	*motorway junction*
das Autobahnkreuz	*motorway intersection*
Stau auf der Autobahn	*traffic jam on the motorway*
Abstand halten	*keep your distance*
die Geschwindigkeitsbegrenzung	*speed restriction*
das Überholverbot	*no overtaking*
die Umleitung	*diversion*
zwischen	*between*
Wo stehen Sie?	*Where are you?*
Ich bin auf der A1 bei	*I'm on the A1 near*
Delmenhorst Richtung	*Delmenhorst going towards*
Hamburg.	*Hamburg.*

Achtung!	*warning*	**die Raststätte**	*services*
Richtung	*direction*	**in der Nähe von/bei**	*near*
die Baustelle	*road works*	**der Nebel**	*fog*
das Glatteis	*ice*	**die Rutschgefahr**	*danger of skidding*

Exercise 1

How would you ask someone to:
- i   check the tyre pressures?
- ii   clean the windscreen?
- iii   check the oil?

Exercise 2

What do these signs mean? Match each sign with its meaning.

a car park   **b** one-way street   **c** motorway exit
d petrol station   **e** motorway services with restaurant
f way on to the motorway

i

ii

iii

vi

v

iv

Learning note

- Practise saying all the new words and phrases.

Exercise 3

How would you tell someone you are ...?

a on the A4 between Cologne (Köln) and Aachen travelling towards Aachen.

b near Solingen travelling towards Dortmund on the A1.

c on the A5 near Offenburg travelling towards Basel.

d on the A8 near Augsburg travelling to Munich (München).

e on the B10 near Geislingen between Stuttgart and Ulm, travelling towards Ulm.

▶ Listening exercise 30

Where is the motorway blocked?

ℹ️ Motorway signs are blue and white and the motorways are numbered A1, A2, etc. The European equivalent numbers are prefixed with 'E'.

The motorways which link up with international routes also have European numbers which are in green. If the two numbers are different this can be confusing. It is usually easier to ignore the green signs and follow the blue ones.

Signs on the **Bundesstraßen** trunk roads are in yellow and black.

Distances are given in *kilometres* (**Kilometer**).

To convert miles to kilometres:

> divide by 5 and multiply the answer by 8
> 20 miles ÷ 5 = 4 × 8 = 32 km

To convert kilometres to miles:

> divide by 8 and multiply the answer by 5
> 80 km ÷ 8 = 10 × 5 = 50 miles

Stau auf der Autobahn *Congestion on the motorway*

This is the sort of message you might hear on the car radio warning you about traffic problems ahead.

> Durch einen Unfall ist die Autobahn bei Friedberg blockiert. Der Stau ist 11 Kilometer lang. Reisende nach München werden gebeten, die Autobahn bei Augsburg zu verlassen und die Bundesstraße 2 zu benutzen.

zu verlassen	*to leave*		
die Bundesstraße	*trunk road* (lit: federal road)		
durch	*through*	**bei**	*near, at*
blockiert	*blocked*	**Reisende**	*travellers*
nach München	*to Munich*	**werden gebeten**	*are asked*
zu benutzen	*to use*	**der Unfall**	*accident*

Exercise 4

Read the passage and see if you can answer the questions:

a Where is the motorway blocked?
b Why is it blocked?
c Where should those travelling to Munich leave the motorway?
d What road should they use instead?

Strassenschilder *Street signs*

Umleitung
(diversion)

Vorfahrtstraße
(this road has the
right of way)

Baustelle
(road works)

i When driving in Germany always have your **Führerschein/ Fahrzeugschein** *driving licence* with you. If driving a hire car, you also need the vehicle registration document.

In towns there is a speed limit of 50 km/h (sometimes 30 km/h). On other roads it is 100 km/h but there is no overall limit on the motorways although there are sometimes local restrictions.

Germans tend to drive very fast and very close on the motorways, but they are usually strict about obeying speed limits where they exist. There are a lot of radar checks and if you are caught speeding you will be expected to pay the fine on the spot.

You must used dipped headlights if visibility is poor. Fog lights may only be used when visibility is less than 50 metres. If you break down you must display a red warning triangle about 100 metres behind your car.

Ich habe eine Panne *My car has broken down*

Ich habe eine Panne.	*My car has broken down.*
Ich habe einen Unfall gehabt.	*I have had an accident.*
Was für ein Auto haben Sie?	*What kind of a car have you got?*
Welche Automarke haben Sie?	*What make of car is it?*
das Kennzeichen	*car registration*
Können Sie das Auto reparieren?	*Can you repair the car?*
Was ist los?	*What is wrong?*
Das Benzin ist alle.	*I have run out of petrol.*
Mein/e … ist kaputt.	*My … is broken.*
Sind Sie Mitglied eines Autovereins?	*Are you a member of an automobile club?*

i On the motorways there is an emergency phone (**Notrufsäule**) every two kilometres. This will connect you with the nearest motorway control unit.

If you have to make a call on one you will probably be asked:

- your registration number
- what number phone you are calling from
- what road you are on
- what direction you are travelling in

Exercise 5
What are you being asked?

a Was ist los?   **b** Was für ein Auto haben Sie?

c Wo stehen Sie?   d Welche Automarke haben Sie?
e Sind Sie Mitglied eines Automobilclubs?

▶ Listening exercise 31

What has happened to these seven motorists?

▶ Dialogue 36

Sie	Autobahnhilfe
Ich habe eine Panne.	
	Wo stehen Sie?
Ich bin auf der A8 in der Nähe von Rosenheim Richtung Salzburg.	
	Bei welchem Autobahn-kilometer stehen Sie?
115.	
	Was für ein Auto haben Sie?
Einen Volkswagen Golf.	
	Kennzeichen?
GWY 622.	
	Was ist los?
Der Motor wird zu heiß.	
	Sind Sie Mitglied eines Autovereins?
Ja. AA.	
	Wie ist Ihre Mitgliedsnummer?
Das weiß ich im Moment nicht. Mein Ausweis ist im Auto.	
	Ok. Jemand kommt gleich.
Wann wird er hier sein?	
	In zwanzig Minuten.

Learning notes

- Make sure you understand both parts of the dialogue.
- Practise reading your part of the conversation.

- Now vary it to say:
  - you are on the A7 between Hannover and Hamburg travelling towards Hamburg, phone number 87.
  - you have a Ford Sierra, J 123 QWE.
  - you are a member of the AA (your membership number is 16 5653 3789).
  - your windscreen is broken.

Wo kann ich hier parken? *Where can I park?*

die Parkuhr	*parking meter*
der Parkplatz	*car park*
die Tiefgarage	*underground garage* (lit: deep garage)
das Parkhaus	*multi-storey car park*
der Parkschein	*parking ticket*
die Parkgebühr	*parking fee*
Parkverbot	*parking forbidden*
die Einbahnstraße	*one-way street*
die Ampel	*traffic lights*
biegen	*to turn*
Hier dürfen Sie nicht parken.	*You can't park here.*
Hier ist Parkverbot.	*Parking is forbidden here.*
Wie komme ich zum Parkplatz?	*How do I get to the car park?*
Hier dürfen Sie nicht fahren.	*You can't go/drive here.*
Es ist eine Einbahnstraße.	*It's a one-way street.*
Anlieger frei	*Residents only*
Fussgängerzone	*pedestrian area*
Spielstraße	*children may be playing*
Kennzeichen	*registration number(s)*

i You usually have to pay fines for illegal parking, as for speeding, on the spot.

Exercise 6

You're about to park your car in the street, when you're approached by a traffic policeman. Complete your part of the conversation.

Polizist	**Hier dürfen Sie nicht parken.**
a **You**	*Ask where you can park.*

Polizist	**Es gibt ein Parkhaus vor dem Bahnhof.**
b **You**	*Ask how to get to the station.*
Polizist	**Sie biegen hier gleich links ab, dann geradeaus bis zur Ampel, dann links und wieder links.**
c **You**	*Ask where you can park.*
Passant	**Der Parkplatz ist voll. Sie müssen in der Tiefgarage einen Platz finden.**
d **You**	*Ask where it is.*
Passant	**Gegenüber der Stadthalle.**
e **You**	*Ask if it is expensive.*
Passant	**Ein Euro pro Stunde bis 20.00 Uhr.**
f **You**	*And after 8.00pm?*
Passant	**Nichts.**
g **You**	*Ask if he/she has any change.*
Passant	**Was brauchen Sie?**
h **You**	*Two 50 cent coins.*
Passant	**Nein, leider nicht. Sie müssen zum Kiosk gehen.**

Exercise 7

Who can park in these places?

i You can tell where a German car is registered by the first letter or letters on the number plate, for example:

B	Berlin	**BN**	Bonn	**D**	Düsseldorf	**DO**	Dortmund
H	Hannover	**HH**	Hamburg	**M**	München	**MR**	Marburg
L	Leipzig						

19

was ist mit Ihnen los?

what's wrong with you?

In this unit you will learn how to
- say you don't feel well and ask for medicine
- understand the instructions on the bottle
- find out about opening times

Was ist mit Ihnen los? *What's the matter with you?*

Ich fühle mich nicht wohl.	*I don't feel well*
Ich habe ...	*I have ...*
Ich habe Kopfschmerzen	*I have headache* (lit: head pains)
Ich habe Ohrenschmerzen	*I have earache*
Ich habe Zahnschmerzen	*I have toothache*
Ich habe Halsschmerzen	*I have sore throat*
Ich habe einen Sonnenbrand	*I have sunburn*
Ich habe eine Grippe	*I have flu*
Ich habe eine Erkältung	*I have a cold*
Ich habe Heuschnupfen	*I have hay fever*
Ich habe eine Allergie	*I have an allergy*
Ich habe Husten	*I have a cough*
Ich habe Fieber	*I have a temperature*
Ich habe Durchfall	*I have diarrhoea*
Mein Bein tut weh.	*My leg hurts.*
Ich bin schlechter Laune.	*I am in a bad mood.*
Arm	*arm*
Fuß	*foot*
Magen	*stomach*
meine Hand	*hand*
Gesundheit!	*Bless you!* (lit: health)
gesund	*well, healthy*
krank	*sick, ill*
Haben Sie ein Mittel gegen ...?	*Have you got something for ...?*
Tabletten	*tablets*
schmerzstillende Tabletten	*painkillers*
Zäpfchen	*suppositories*
eine Salbe	*cream, ointment*
Hustentropfen	*liquid cough medicine* (lit. cough drops) *(to put in water)*
Hustenbonbons	*cough sweets (to suck)*

Exercise 1

How would you say the following?

a You have a cold.
b You don't feel well.
c Have you got something for sunburn?
d How often should I take them?
e You have a cough.
f You have toothache.

▶ Listening exercise 32

Was ist mit ihnen los? *What is wrong with these four people?*

In der Apotheke *At the chemist's*

Exercise 2

a **You**	*Tell the chemist that you don't feel well.*	
Apothekerin	Was ist mit Ihnen los?	
b **You**	*Say you've got a temperature. You've got a headache and a sore throat.*	
Apothekerin	Ach, Sie haben eine Grippe. Ich gebe Ihnen Tabletten gegen Halsschmerzen.	
c **You**	*Ask her if she has anything for the headache.*	
Apothekerin	Gegen Fieber nimmt man am besten Aspirin.	

Exercise 3

Wie oft soll ich sie einnehmen? *How often should I take them?*

See if you can match each instruction with one of the labelled medicines overleaf.

a Every four hours with water.
b Three times a day as required.
c One tablet twice a day.
d After meals, twice a day.
e Every three hours.
f Apply/rub in as required.

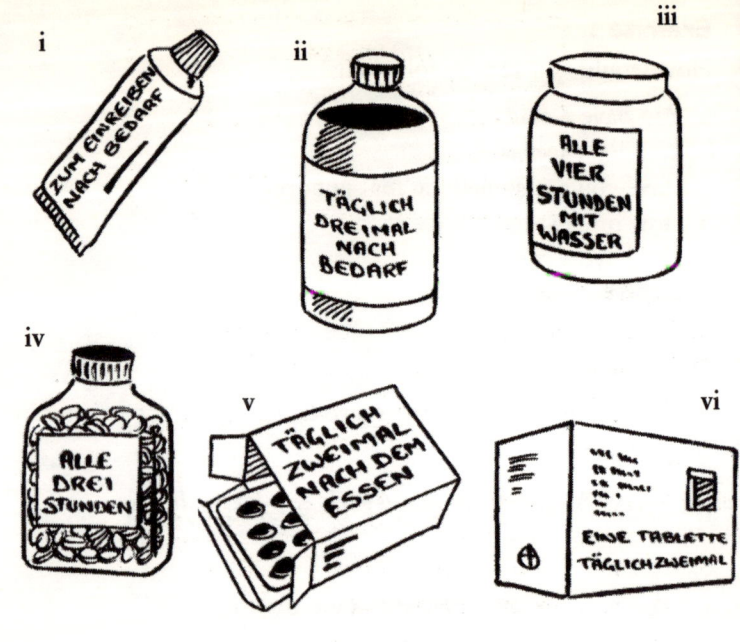

i ZUM EINREIBEN NACH BEDARF

ii TÄGLICH DREIMAL NACH BEDARF

iii ALLE VIER STUNDEN MIT WASSER

iv ALLE DREI STUNDEN

v TÄGLICH ZWEIMAL NACH DEM ESSEN

vi EINE TABLETTE TÄGLICH ZWEIMAL

i You will receive free medical treatment at doctors' surgeries and hospitals if you have the European Health Insurance Card which is available from your local post office. Nearly all Germans have some form of private health insurance.

Geschäftszeiten *Opening times*

Wann?	*When?*
Um wie viel Uhr?	*At what time?*
der Ruhetag	*closing day* (lit: *rest day*)
Betriebsferien	*works/shop holiday*
der Feierabend	*end of the working day*
Öffnungszeiten	*opening times*
offen/geöffnet	*open*
geschlossen	*closed*
um	*at (time)*

> **Öffnungszeiten**
> Montag–Mittwoch u. Freitag
> 8.30–13.00 Uhr u. 14.15–16.00 Uhr
> Donnerstag
> 8.30–13.00 Uhr u. 14.15–18.00 Uhr

Exercise 4

a When is the chemists open on a Thursday?
b When is the chemists open on a Monday?
c Is the chemists open on a Saturday?

Exercise 5

How would you tell your German friend:
a when the chemists are open where you live?
  i Am ... ist die Apotheke von ... Uhr bis ... geöffnet.
  ii Am ... ist die Apotheke nicht geöffnet.

b when you finish work?
  Wann haben Sie Feierabend?
  Um ... Uhr ist für mich Feierabend.

c which day the shops are closed where you live?
  Welcher Tag ist Ruhetag?
  _____ ist hier Ruhetag.

d what time the shops usually shut?
  die Geschäfte machen meistens um ... Uhr zu.

▶ Dialogue 37

Sie	**Freund**
Bitte, gibt es eine Apotheke in der Nähe?	
	Ja, in der Hauptstraße, aber sie ist im Moment geschlossen.
Wann wird sie geöffnet?	
	Um 14.00 Uhr.

Bis wann?

Bis 16.30 Uhr.

Danke.

Bitte.

Exercise 6

Put your part of this dialogue into German, then read through the whole dialogue out loud and check you understand it all.

a	**You**	*You want to go to buy some medicine. Ask if there is a chemists nearby.*
	Freund	Sie ist im Moment geschlossen.
b	**You**	*Ask when it will open.*
	Freund	Um 14.00 Uhr.
c	**You**	*Ask when it shuts again.*
	Freund	Um 16.30 Uhr.

Learning note

- Revise telling the time. How do you say these times?

| 10.15 | 2.30 | 14.45 | 3.05 |
| 6.20 | 17.40 | 11.30 | 12.00 |

Exercise 7

a When is this shop open?

b And when is this one not open?

Öffnungszeiten

Montag bis Freitag
8.45–18.30 Uhr
Samstag 8.45–13.00 Uhr
la. Samstag 8.45–18.00 Uhr

Betriebsferien

14.–28. Juli

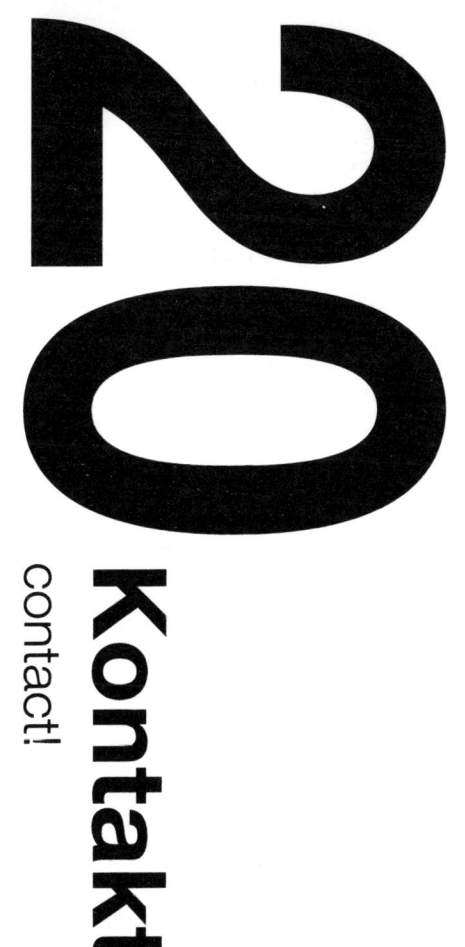

20

Kontakt!

contact!

In this unit you will learn how to

- keep in contact using a computer and a mobile phone
- ask for help with using your computer
- make arrangements

der PC oder der Computer	*PC or computer*
der Laptop	*laptop*
die Festplatte	*hard drive*
der Server	*server*
die Tastatur	*keyboard*
die Maus	*mouse*
der Speicher Stick	*memory stick*
die Akte	*file*
das E-Mail	*email*
die CD	*CD*
die Überspielbare CD	*re-writeable CD*
Wireless LAN / Drahtlos	*WIFI*
Alle Computer sind ausser Dienst.	*All the computers are down.*
Keine Verbindung zum Internet.	*The internet is down.*

Ich möchte ...	*I would like to ...*
meine E-Mails herunterladen	*download my emails*
ein E-Mail versenden	*send an email*
eine Anlage dazu versenden	*send an attachment*
eine Anlage sichern	*save an attachment*
eine Akte entfernen/löschen	*delete a file*
eine Akte kopieren	*copy a file*
meinen Laptop anschliessen	*connect my laptop*
in Internet surfen	*surf the internet*
in meine Mailbox	*get into my mailbox*
einen Stadtplan ausdrucken	*print a plan of the town*
in Google surfen	*(to) google (something)*
den Zugfahrplan ansehen	*look up train times*
einen Flug buchen	*book a flight*
ein Hotel suchen	*look for a hotel*
ein Foto versenden	*send a photo*
die Wettervorhersage heraussuchen	*look up the weather forecast*
ein Podcast herunterladen	*download a podcast*
das Abendprogramm ansehen	*find out what is on tonight*

What other things might you want to do on the computer?
Here are some suggestions.

das **Internetcafé**	*internet café*
der **Internetanschluss**	*internet connection*
Wo kann ich den	*Where can I use it (internet*
(Internetanschluss) benutzen?	*connection)?*
das **USB-Kabel**	*USB cable*
den **Versand vornehmen**	*to send*
selbstverständlich	*of course*

▶ **Dialogue 38**

Sie	**Empfangsdame**
Ist hier in der Nähe ein Internetcafé?	
	Nein, aber das Hotel hat einen Internetanschluss.
Wo kann ich den benutzen?	
	Ein Anschluss ist in Ihrem Zimmer. Dort können Sie Ihr Laptop anschliessen oder Sie gehen in das Business Center und benutzen einen PC von uns.
Was kostet das?	
	€5,00 die Stunde.
Wie kann ich eine Akte über meinen PC versenden? Ich habe mein USB-Kabel nicht mit.	
	Haben Sie einen Speicher Stick?
Ja!	
	Dann können Sie den Versand über den Hotel-Computer vornehmen.
Kann ich es auch ausdrucken?	
	Ja, selbstverständlich.

Exercise 1

Match the German phrases to their English equivalents.

a Ich komme nicht ins Internet, was muss ich tun?
b Haben Sie 'senden' angeklickt?
c Ich kann diese Akte nicht herunterladen.
d Es liegt eine Störung vor.
e Gehen Sie bitte an einen anderen PC.

i I can't download this file.
ii There is a problem.
iii I can't get onto the web, what should I do?
iv Please use another PC.
v Have you clicked on 'send'?

▶ Listening exercise 33

Was wollen sie machen? *What do they want to do?*

Wann treffen wir uns? *When shall we meet?*

ℹ In German a mobile phone is usually referred to as **ein Handy**.

▶ Dialogue 39

Sie	Ein Kollege
Können Sie mich heute Abend anrufen?	
	Wie ist Ihre Telefonnummer?
Sie brauchen die Ländervorwahl für Deutschland, +49, und meine Telefonnummer ohne die Null.	
	Welche Telefonnummer haben Sie?
Also +49 für Deutschland; Hamburg hat die Vorwahl 040, ohne Null heisst es +49 40, und meine Telefonnummer... 1 23 45 67 89.	
	Wie ist Ihre Handynummer?
+49 für Deutschland, dann 171 98 76 54 32, aber wo ich wohne gibt es nicht immer Funkkontakt. Falls es keinen Funkkontakt gibt, rufen Sie mich auf dem Festnetz an.	
	O.K. In Ordnung. Bis dann.
Tschüss.	

21

Geschäftsreise oder Besuch?

business trip or visit?

In this unit you will learn how to
- make more detailed arrangements for accommodation
- read signs about the town
- ask the way to somewhere complicated
- ask for things and say if something is wrong in more detail
- read the signs at a trade fair
- recognize the Länder

Haben Sie ein Zimmer frei? *Have you a room available?*

$$\boxed{\textit{Zimmer}}$$

ℹ Übernachtung *Accommodation*

The town information bureau **Auskunftsbüro/Verkehrsamt** (or the organizers of the trade fair or conference) can help you find accommodation.

It is possible to stay in private houses and this is usually much cheaper than in hotels.

Zimmernachweis is where you can ask about rooms available.

die Messe	*trade fair*
das Hotel	*a hotel (usually international standard)*
das Gasthaus } **der Gasthof** }	*a hotel, often typical of the region, inn*
die Pension	*a cheaper hotel*
Zimmer frei	*rooms vacant*
Zimmer belegt } **Zimmer besetzt** }	*rooms taken no vacancies*
Wie komme ich zum/zur …?	*How do I get to the …?*
Vollpension *full board*	**Halbpension** *half board*
zu teuer *too dear*	**das Zimmer** *room*

Exercise 1

What do these signs mean?

Zimmer frei

Zimmer belegt

Zimmernachweis

Exercise 2

Match the sign to the facilities:

a   e   i   m

b   f   j   n

c   g   k   o

d   h   l   p

1 Restaurant	7 Schwimmbad	12 Konferenzraum
2 Parkplatz	8 Doppelzimmer	13 Kreditkarten
3 Fax	9 Einzelzimmer	14 Sauna
4 Airport-transfer	10 Garage	15 Für Behinderte geeignet
5 Telefon	11 Bar	16 Fernseher
6 Frühstücksbüffet		

▶ Dialogue 40

Sie	Empfangsdame
Haben Sie noch ein Zimmer frei?	
	Einzel- oder Doppelzimmer?
Ein Einzelzimmer.	
	Mit Bad oder Dusche?
Mit Dusche. Haben Sie ein Zimmer mit Telefon?	
	Ja. Im Hotel Superdeluxe. €180 pro Nacht.
Das ist zu teuer.	
	Pension Sailer. Ein Einzelzimmer mit Bad kostet €50 inklusive Frühstück.
Gibt es einen Parkplatz?	
	Nein. Aber Sie können bis 8.00 Uhr auf der Straße parken.

Gut. Ich nehme es. Wie komme ich am besten zur Pension?

Sie fahren hier geradeaus und dann links. Die Pension Sailer ist auf der rechten Seite.

Vielen Dank. Auf Wiedersehen.

Learning note

• Practise the dialogue, reading both parts out loud.

Ich bin zur Messe hier *I have come to the trade fair*

Ankommen *Getting there*

Here are some phrases that might be useful.

Wie komme ich zur Messe?	*How do I get to the fair?*
mit der Straßenbahn Linie ...	*(with) tram number ...*
mit der U-Bahn	*(on the) underground*
mit dem Bus	*(on the) bus*
Wo ist die Haltestelle?	*Where is the stop?*
Wo ist die U-Bahnstation?	*Where is the underground station?*
die Fahrkarte	*ticket*
zu Fuß	*on foot*
Ist es weit?	*Is it far?*
Es ist gerade um die Ecke	*It's just round the corner*
Wie oft fährt der Bus?/die U-Bahn?	*How often does the bus/ underground run?*
alle 20 Minuten	*every 20 minutes*
Wo treffen wir uns?	*Where shall we meet?*
Wann treffen wir uns?	*When shall we meet?*
der Treffpunkt	*the meeting place*
eine Eintrittskarte	*an entry ticket*
Ich bin Aussteller.	*I am an exhibitor.*
Ich bin Einkäufer/in.	*I am a buyer.*
Meine Firma heißt ...	*My firm is called ...*

Exercise 3

Pair up the question words.

i	Wo?	a	When?
ii	Wann?	b	Which?
iii	Was?	c	How much ...?
iv	Was für ...?	d	How?
v	Wie viel ...?	e	Where?
vi	Welcher?	f	Who?
vii	Wie?	g	What kind of ...?
viii	Wer?	h	What?

i If you are travelling by car and want to take it to the fair every day you will find it very helpful to book parking in advance.

Remember to drive on the right and to adapt your headlights accordingly.

▶ Exercise 4

Complete your part of the dialogue, and then read the whole dialogue out loud, checking that you understand it all.

a	**You**	*How do I get to the fair?*
	Freund	Mit dem Bus oder mit der U-Bahn?
b	**You**	*Which bus?*
	Freund	Linie 14.
c	**You**	*How often does it run?*
	Freund	Alle zwanzig Minuten.
d	**You**	*Which U-Bahn?*
	Freund	Linie 3 und Linie 5.
e	**You**	*Do I have to change?*
	Freund	Ja. Sie steigen am Bahnhof um.
f	**You**	*How often does it run?*
	Freund	Alle zehn Minuten.
		Die U-Bahn ist schneller.
g	**You**	*Thank you.*

You arrive, but you haven't booked your ticket in advance ...

h	**You**	*Say you would like an entrance ticket.*
	Beamter	Einkäufer oder Aussteller?

i	**You**	*You are a buyer.*
Beamter		Name und Firma?
j	**You**	*Give your details.*
Beamter		Unterschreiben Sie hier.
		Das kostet €10.

In der Messehalle *At the trade fair*

Wo bekommt man ...?	*Where can you get ...?*
Wo bekommt man einen Aschenbecher?	*Where can you get an ashtray?*
Wo bekommt man Wasser?	*Where can you get water?*
Wo bekommt man Blumen?	*Where can you get flowers?*
Wo bekommt man Getränke?	*Where can you get drinks?*
Wo bekommt man einen Imbiss?	*Where can you get a snack?*
Wo bekommt man ein Programm?	*Where can you get a programme?*
Wo bekommt man einen Schlüssel für Stand Nr ...?	*Where can you get a key for stand no. ...?*
Wo kann ich Fotokopien machen?	*Where can I get photocopies?*
Wo kann ich ein Fax abschicken?	*Where can I send a fax?*
Wo sind die Toiletten?	*Where are the toilets?*
Mein Telefon/Kühlschrank ist kaputt.	*My telephone/fridge doesn't work.*
Ich habe keinen Strom.	*I have no electricity.*
Ich habe kein Telefon.	*I have no telephone.*
Ich habe kein Wasser.	*I have no water.*
Ich habe ein Telefon bestellt.	*I ordered a telephone.*

Exercise 5

Complete your part of the dialogue.

a	**You**	*Say you want the key for your stand.*
Hallenmeister		Welche Nummer?
b	**You**	*21.*
Hallenmeister		Bitte schön.
c	**You**	*The electricity doesn't work.*
Hallenmeister		Ich schicke den Elektriker.

d You *Where can you get ashtrays?*

Hallenmeister Im Kiosk.

e You *Where can you get water?*

Hallenmeister Es gibt einen Wasserhahn in der Ecke.

▶ Listening exercise 34

Wo? *Where?*

a Where can you get photocopies?
b Where can you get a meal?
c Where can you get drinks?
d Where are the toilets?
e Where is the nearest phone?

der Eingang	*entrance*
der Ausgang	*exit*
die Halle	*exhibition hall*
die Rolltreppe	*escalator*
der Aufzug/Fahrstuhl	*lift*
das Restaurant	*restaurant*
der Pendelbus	*shuttle bus service*
Erste Hilfe	*first aid*
der Hallenmeister	*hall caretaker*

Exercise 6

Which sign is which?

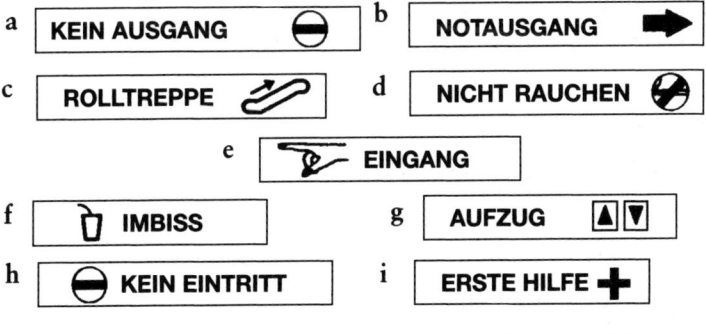

a KEIN AUSGANG ⊖
b NOTAUSGANG ➡
c ROLLTREPPE ⤴
d NICHT RAUCHEN 🚭
e ☞ EINGANG
f 🗑 IMBISS
g AUFZUG ▲▼
h ⊖ KEIN EINTRITT
i ERSTE HILFE ✚

i   entrance
ii   snack bar
iii lift

iv   emergency exit
v   escalator
vi   no entry

vii no smoking
viii no exit
ix   first aid

In der Stadt *In the town*

What do the signs tell you?

RADFAHREN IM PARK
NICHT GESTATTET

BETRETEN DER
BAUSTELLE VERBOTEN

RASEN NICHT
BETRETEN

ACHTUNG
FAHRZEUGVERKEHR
VON RECHTS

RAUCHEN VERBOTEN

FUSSGÄNGERWEG
GEGENÜBER BENUTZEN

ACHTUNG
SCHRANKE

EINTRITT
VERBOTEN

nicht gestattet	*not permitted*
nicht erlaubt	*not allowed*
verboten	*forbidden*
untersagt	*not allowed*
Achtung!	*warning*
Betreten	*walking on*
die Baustelle	*building site*
der Rasen	*grass* (lit: lawn)
Fahrzeugverkehr	*traffic*
die Schranke	*level crossing barrier*
Vorsicht!	*Be careful! Watch out!*
der Fußgängerweg	*pavement*
gegenüber	*opposite*
benutzen	*to use*

Land *Region*	Hauptstadt *Capital city*
Baden-Württemburg	Stuttgart
Bayern	München
Berlin	Berlin
Brandenburg	Potsdam
Bremen	Bremen
Hamburg	Hamburg
Hessen	Wiesbaden
Mecklenburg-Vorpommern	Schwerin
Niedersachsen	Hannover
Nordrhein-Westfalen	Düsseldorf
Rheinland-Pfalz	Mainz
Saarland	Saarbrücken
Sachsen	Dresden
Sachsen-Anhalt	Magdeburg
Schleswig-Holstein	Kiel
Thüringen	Erfurt

Die Länder *The regions*

The Federal Republic of Germany consists of 16 regions (**Bundesländer**). Each **Land** (plural **Länder**) has its own regional parliament (**Landtag**) with much jurisdiction over regional affairs. Each **Land** or group of **Länder** has summer holidays at a different time on a rota so that not everyone is on the move at once.

Kiel

SCHLESWIG-HOLSTEIN

Hamburg   Schwerin

HAMBURG   MECKLENBURG-VORPOMMERN

Bremen   BREMEN

NIEDERSACHSEN   BRANDENBURG

Hannover   Berlin

BERLIN

SACHSEN-   Potsdam
ANHALT

Düsseldorf   Magdeburg

NORDRHEIN-
WESTFALEN   SACHSEN

Erfurt   Dresden

HESSEN   THÜRINGEN

RHEINLAND-   Wiesbaden
PFALZ

Mainz

SAARLAND

Saarbrücken

Stuttgart   BAYERN

BADEN-WÜRTTEMBERG

München

Congratulations on completing *Teach Yourself Beginner's German*!

I hope you have enjoyed working your way through the course. I am always keen to receive feedback from people who have used my course, so why not contact me and let me know your reactions? I always welcome comments and suggestions and I do my best to incorporate constructive suggestions into later editions.

You can contact me through the publishers at:

Teach Yourself Books, Hodder Headline Ltd, 338 Euston Road, London NW1 3BH.

I hope you will want to build on your knowledge of German and have made a few suggestions to help you do this in the section entitled **Taking it further**.

Alles Gute!

Rosi McNab

taking it further

If you have enjoyed working your way through *Teach Yourself Beginner's German* and want to take your German further, why not try *Teach Yourself German*? You should find it ideal for building on your existing knowledge and improving your listening, reading and writing skills.

The following websites will help you take further your knowledge of German and the German-speaking world:

http://www.goethe.de The *Goethe Institut* is represented in most countries and staff may be able to inform you about German language courses in your area. They will also have information on short intensive courses based in Germany.

http://www.austria.org for information about Austrian life and culture.

http://www.swissinfo.org for information about Swiss life and culture.

Try some real German!

Have a go at listening to German-speaking radio and TV stations and reading German newspapers and magazines.

Whatever you try, it's best to concentrate on small extracts at first – either a video or audio clip or a short article. See how much you can work out, going over the material several times. Then look up any key words that you have not understood, and go on till you are satisfied that you have grasped the main ideas. If you do this on a regular basis, you'll find that your command of German increases steadily.

Sources of real German

- Newspapers, magazines (e.g. *Bild-Zeitung*, *Stern*, *Focus*).
- Satellite and cable TV channels (e.g. ARD, RTL, SAT1, ZDF).
- Radio stations via satellite and, within Europe, on Medium Wave after dark.
- Internet – most German newspapers have websites where you can browse for short articles that interest you. TV and radio stations, too, have websites where you can often find audio and video clips of the latest newscasts. In some cases you will also find transcripts of the newscasts to help you if you run into difficulties with the spoken language. Use a German-language search engine or portal such as http://www.google.de, http://de.yahoo.com or http://www.tiscali.de to find any of the above and lots more besides.
- Last but not least, we would highly recommend that you try speaking German with native-speakers, whether in your home country or in a German-speaking country. Explore Berlin, Vienna or Zürich (or any other German-speaking city) and make contact with the locals!

Viel Spaß beim Weiterlernen!

key to the exercises

Unit 1

1 a Guten Tag b auch c Herr d auf Wiedersehen e gut f Es geht mir gut g vielen Dank h Wie geht es Ihnen? i und 2 a geht b heiße c mir d Wiedersehen **Listening exercise 1** 1 iia 2 iiib 3 iva 4 ia 5 ic 6 ivb 7 iib 8 iiic 3a Wie heißen Sie? b Ich verstehe nicht c Ich heiße d Entschuldigen Sie bitte e morgen f Herr Schulz ist nicht da g Auf Wiedersehen h Wie bitte? i ein bisschen **Revision** 1 a Guten Morgen b Guten Tag c Guten Tag d Guten Abend 2 c 3 c 4 i vee gate es ee-nen ii unt iii dankuh iv hair v frow vi ow-uch vii owf-veeder-say-un. 5 a Sie b bitte c verstehe d heiße, heißen f nicht g Auf h bisschen 6 a ii b i c iv d iii **Listening exercise 2** a iii b ii c ii d i

Unit 2

1 a Tee mit Milch b Kaffee c Kaffee mit Milch d Kaffee mit Sahne e Zitronentee mit Zucker f Apfelsaft g Orangensaft h Tomatensaft i eine Dose Fanta j eine Flasche Cola 2 a travel agents b traveller's cheques c travel costs d lemon tea 3 a ein Glas Zitronentee b ein Glas Rotwein c Kaffee mit Sahne d Tee mit Milch und Zucker e Bier f ein Glas Weißwein g Orangensaft **Revision** 1 a Wie war die Reise? b Trinken Sie … c Trinken Sie Kaffee mit Milch und Zucker? d Essen Sie ein Stück Kuchen? 2 a iv b i c iii d v e ii

Listening exercise 3 a i b ii c i d iii **Listening exercise 4** a i b ii c iii **Sign language 1** cup or pot of coffee (also decaffeinated available), mocha drink, cup or pot of $1/2$ hot chocolate and $1/2$ coffee, cup or pot of hot chocolate, pot of hot chocolate with cream, pot of tea, cup of tea with rum, glass of camomile or peppermint tea 2 Bringen Sie mir einen Kaffee, einen Tee, ein Bier, eine Cola, bitte

Unit 3

1 eins; zwei; drei; vier; fünf; sechs; sieben; acht; neun; zehn; elf; zwölf; dreizehn; vierzehn; fünfzehn; sechzehn; siebzehn; achtzehn; neunzehn; zwanzig 2 eins; dreizehn; sieben; zwei; fünf; elf; acht; neun; siebzehn; sechs; vier; achtzehn; zwanzig; drei 3 a vier b sechs c drei d zwei e fünf f zwei 4 a fünf Glas Rotwein b drei Glas Weißwein c sechs Tassen Tee d drei Tassen Kaffee e vier Flaschen Bier f zwei Dosen Cola **Listening exercise 5** 1–15 2–5 3–7 4–16 5–10 6–13 7–19 8–3 9–20 10–1 11–17 12–4 5 a einundzwanzig b fünfundzwanzig c zweiunddreißig d sechsunddreißig e dreiundvierzig f siebenundvierzig g vierundfünfzig h achtundfünfzig i einundsechzig j neunundsechzig k zweiundsiebzig l fünfundsiebzig m vierundachtzig n achtundachtzig o zweiundneunzig p neunundneunzig.

Listening exercise 6 1–32 2–36 3–54 4–21 5–88 6–92 7–25 8–72 9–69 10–43 11–84 12–47 13–58 14–99 15–75 16–61 Listening exercise 7 a 24 b 23 c 52 d 46 e 83 f 67 g 93 h 92 i 84 j 62 Revision: Listening exercise 8 a €5,20 b €12,80 c €16,50 d €43,60 e €50,00 f €4,75 g €40,10 h €54,00 i €25,00 j €27,90 1 a zwei Tassen Tee b drei Flaschen Bier c fünf Glas Rotwein d vier Stück Kuchen e acht Glas Weißwein

Unit 4

1 a Wie geht es Ihnen? b Wann kommen Sie nach London? c Was machen Sie morgen? d Spielen Sie gern Tennis? e Schwimmen Sie gern? f Trinken Sie gern eine Tasse Kaffee? 2 a l g e m h 3 a du b Wie geht es dir? c Trinkst du gern eine Tasse Kaffee oder ein Glas Orangensaft? Listening exercise 9 1 du 2 Sie 3 Sie 4 du 5 Sie 6 Sie 7 du 8 Ihnen/Sie 9 du 10 du Listening exercise 10 1 Friedrich Bittner 2 Ilse Egeberg 3 Reinhard Drexler 4 Wolf Kasselmann 5 Hans Kauffeld 6 Renate Walkemeier Listening exercise 11 i Braunschweig ii Heidelberg iii Wuppertal-Romsdorf iv Iserlohn v Offenbach vi Passau vii Magdeburg viii Erfurt ix Cuxhafen x Karlsruhe xi Mittenwald xii Ingolstadt Revision 1a l b f c a d r e t f h g m h g 2 a Wie heißt du? b Woher kommst du? c Trinkst du gern ein Glas Limonade? d Spielst du gern Tennis mit John? 3 a st b en c en d st e en f st g st h en i st j en k st l en Quiz 1 c 2 b 3 c 4 c 5 a 6 b 7 a 8 a Munich; b Cologne; c Stuttgart; d Vienna 9 a Rhine b Moselle c Danube d die Zugspitze is the highest mountain in Germany 10 a 11 see map page 206

Unit 5

1 a Deutschland b Frankreich c Italien d Polen e Irland f Großbritannien g Belgien h Spanien i Österreich j England k Schottland l Holland m Portugal n die Schweiz o Wales Listening exercise 12 1 German from Stuttgart in Germany 2 Dutch from The Hague in Holland 3 Belgian from Brussels 4 French from Paris 5 Austrian from Vienna 6 Swiss from Zurich 7 Spanish from Madrid 8 Italian from Milan 9 German from Munich 10 Scottish from Glasgow 2 a Helmut b Waldstraße 34, Stuttgart, Germany c Austrian d single e 35 f 12 34 56 g Salzburg h 70597 Listening exercise 13 Name: Anna Hofmann Wohnort: Dortmund, Neuburgring 38 Postleitzahl: 44267 Telefonnummer: 0230 22 34 56 Staatsangehörigkeit: German Familienstand: married with two children Geburtsort: born 28/4/39 in Halle Ausweisnummer: 1984 2124 7D 3 a Haben Sie ein Zimmer frei? b (say your name) c (say where you are from) d (say what nationality you are) e (give your address) f (give your postcode) g (repeat it) h (give your telephone number) i (give the dialling code) j (say thank you) 4 a Wie heißen Sie? b und mit Vornamen? c Staatsangehörigkeit/Nationalität d Wie ist Ihre Adresse? e und die Postleitzahl? f Wie ist Ihre Telefonnummer? g Wie bitte? h Wie ist die Vorwahl?

Unit 6

1 Haben Sie ein ...? a Einzelzimmer mit Dusche b Doppelzimmer mit Bad c Einzelzimmer mit Bad d Doppelzimmer mit Dusche 2 a Wo ist das Zimmer? b Wo ist der Fahrstuhl? b Wo ist das Telefon? Listening exercise 14 i double 3 nights ii 1 single and 1 double 1 night iii 2 doubles with bath for a week iv single with shower for Monday night v room with 1 double and an extra bed for 1 night (25 September) vi double for 2 nights 12 and 13 August 3 a Ich habe ein Zimmer reserviert b (give your name) c nein. Einzelzimmer mit Dusche d Wie bitte? e Gibt es einen

Fahrstuhl? **f** Wann ist Frühstück? **g** Würden Sie mich um sieben Uhr wecken? **h** Haben Sie ein Zimmer frei? **i** Für drei Nächte **j** Doppelzimmer **k** Bad. Gibt es ein Telefon im Zimmer? **l** Was kostet das? **m** Ist Frühstück inbegriffen? **n** Ich möchte zahlen / die Rechnung bitte **o** Achthundertelf. Nehmen Sie Kreditkarten? **p** Eine Quittung, bitte **q** Würden Sie mich wecken? **r** Um sieben Uhr **s** Zweihundert sieben **4 a** Entschuldigen Sie bitte **b** Mein Zimmer ist zu laut **c** Gibt es eine Dusche? **d** Ich nehme es **e** Entschuldigen Sie bitte. **f** Mein Zimmer ist zu heiß. Wie funktioniert die Heizung? **g** Zimmerservice **h** Das Licht/ die Birne ist kaputt **i** Achtundvierzig **j** Zimmerservice/ Zimmerdienst **k** Würden Sie mich um sechs Uhr wecken? **l** Dreiundsechzig. Ich möchte im Zimmer frühstücken. **m** Um sieben Uhr **5 a** Ich möchte nach England anrufen **b** Ich möchte Zimmer Nummer 25 anrufen **c** Wie mache ich ein Ortsgespräch? **Revision 1** Es gibt **a** kein Telefon **b** keine Bar **c** keinen Fernseher in meinem Zimmer **2** Mein Zimmer ist **a** zu klein **b** zu heiß **c** zu laut **d** zu kalt **3 a** Ich möchte ein Doppelzimmer **b** Ich möchte ein Einzelzimmer mit Dusche **c** Ich möchte ein Familienzimmer **d** Ich möchte ein Zweibettzimmer

Unit 7

1 a sechs Uhr **b** Mittag/zwölf Uhr **c** Viertel nach eins **d** zehn nach zwei **e** zwanzig nach drei **f** Viertel vor fünf **2 a** halb sechs **b** halb acht **c** halb zehn **d** halb zwölf **Listening exercise 15 a** 9.30 **b** 5.30 **c** 7.30 **d** 11.30 **3 a** Wie viel Uhr ist es? **b** Wie viel Uhr ist es? **c** Vielen Dank **d** Auf Wiedersehen **e** Es tut mir Leid. Ich weiß es nicht **4** halb neun; Viertel vor neun; Viertel nach zehn; halb sieben **5 a** Montag Dienstag Mittwoch Donnerstag Freitag Samstag Sonntag **b** 6.00 Uhr morgens; 9.00 Uhr früh; Mittag; 2.00 Uhr nachmittags; 4.00h nachmittags; 6.00h abends; 19.00

Uhr; Mitternacht **6 a** Montag um halb drei nachmittags **b** Donnerstag um elf Uhr nachts **c** Samstag um sieben Uhr abends **d** Dienstag um zehn Uhr zwanzig **e** Sonntag um Viertel vor sechs **f** Mittwoch um halb sechs **g** Freitag um Viertel vor neun **h** Dienstagmittag **i** Donnerstagabend um Viertel nach sechs **7 a** Auf Wiederhören **b** Geht das? **c** Bis dann **d** Ich freue mich schon darauf **Revision 1 a** Es ist sieben Uhr; **b** Viertel nach zwei; **c** halb fünf; **d** Viertel vor zehn; **e** elf Uhr fünfundzwanzig; **f** zehn nach zwölf; **g** acht Uhr fünfunddreißig; **h** zwanzig vor zwei; **i** halb zehn; **j** fünf nach sechs **2 a** Vierzehn Uhr vierundzwanzig; **b** um fünfzehn Uhr siebenundzwanzig; **c** sechzehn Uhr zwölf; **d** neunzehn Uhr neunundzwanzig; **e** zwanzig Uhr einundzwanzig; **f** zweiundzwanzig Uhr zehn; **g** dreizehn Uhr sechsundfünfzig; **h** dreizehn Uhr achtundvierzig **3 a** 4.20 **b** 2.10 **c** 9.30 **d** 10.35 **e** 3.25 **f** 6.35 **g** 8.45 **h** 2.30 **i** 3.45 **j** 8.50 **4 a** vier Uhr; **b** Viertel vor sieben; **c** zwanzig nach zwei; **d** halb elf; **e** fünf Uhr **5 a** Dienstag **b** Freitag **c** Montag **d** Samstag **e** Mittwoch **f** Sonntag **g** Donnerstag **6 a** I need a battery **b** I have lost my watch **c** My watch is broken

Unit 8

1 a Nein. Das ist die Post **b** Dort drüben **c** Bitte/Nichts zu danken **d** Es tut mir Leid. Ich weiß es nicht **e** Dort drüben **f** Auf Wiedersehen **2** der Bahnhof, die Bank, die Bibliothek, die Brücke, das Café, der Flughafen, das Freibad, das Hotel, das Informationsbüro, die Jugendherberge, das Kino, die Kirche, die Kneipe, das Krankenhaus, der Marktplatz, der Park, die Post, das Rathaus, das Reisebüro, das Restaurant, das Schloss, der Schnellimbiss, die Straße **3** Krankenhaus **a** Brücke **b** Kirche **c** Theater **d** Bank **e** Marktplatz **f** Kneipe **g** Kino **h** Flughafen **i** Bahnhof **j** Rathaus **k** Post **Listening exercise 16 1** Nikolai church **2** bank **3** hotel

4 restaurant 5 cinema 6 post office 7 pub 8 station 9 airport 10 information office 4 a Rathausplatz b Bahnhofstraße c Einsteinstraße d Albrecht-Dürer-Allee e Einsteinstraße g Rathausplatz g Rosenheimer Straße h Waldfriedhofallee 5 a in der St-Martins-Straße b in der Rosenheimerstraße c in der Albrecht-Dürer Allee d in der Rosenheimerstraße e in der Einsteinstraße f in der Albrecht-Dürer-Allee g in der Albrecht-Dürer-Allee h in der Albrecht-Dürer-Allee i Waldfriedhofallee j in der Bahnhofstraße k am Rathausplatz l in der Bahnhofstraße m in der Einsteinstraße n in der Albrecht-Dürer-Allee o in der Rosenheimerstraße p in der Bahnhofstraße Revision 1 a xvii b xvi c vii d i e ii f ix g xiii h xix i iv j xii k iii l vi m viii n xviii o x p v q xi r xiv s xv. 2 Campsite; main post office; information office; police station; bus stop; motorway bridge; pedestrian area; main station; sports ground; bus station; petrol station; landing bridge **Listening exercise 17** a r b f c f d r e r f f g f h f i r j f **Sign language** i d ii c iii b iv f v a vi e

Unit 9

1 a zum b zum c zum d zum e zum f zur g zum h zum i zur j zum k zum l zum 2 a geradeaus, auf der rechten Seite b die erste Straße rechts, auf der linken Seite c die zweite Straße links, auf der linken Seite d die erste Straße links, auf der rechten Seite e die zweite Straße rechts, auf der rechten Seite f geradeaus auf der linken Seite 3 Gibt es ... in der Nähe? a einen Bahnhof b einen Campingplatz c eine Post d einen Parkplatz e eine Bank f eine Kneipe g eine Bushaltestelle h ein Hotel 4 a Einzelzimmer mit Dusche b Doppelzimmer mit Bad c Doppelzimmer mit Dusche d Einzelzimmer mit Bad 5 a mit dem Bus b mit dem Auto c mit der Bahn d mit der U-Bahn e zu Fuß 6 a Gibt es ein Hotel in der Nähe? b Haben sie noch Zimmer frei? c Wie komme ich zum Hotel ... zu Fuß; mit dem Auto;

mit dem Bus? 7 a Sie nehmen die erste Straße rechts und X ist auf der linken Seite. b Sie gehen geradeaus bis zur zweiten Straße links und X ist auf der rechten Seite. c Sie gehen geradeaus und X ist auf der linken Seite nach der zweiten Straße links. d Sie nehmen die erste Straße links und X ist auf der rechten Seite. 8 a toilets b hotel c cinema d Rathausplatz e theatre f hospital g post office 9 Wo ist... a die Post b der Bahnhof c die Kirche d die Bank e das Kino f das Hotel g der Supermarkt? Ist es weit? 10 a Hier rechts, gleich links und immer geradeaus b Ja, hier rechts, die erste Straße links, erste Straße rechts, und die Bank ist auf der rechten Seite c Die Post ist gegenüber vom Restaurant d Das Kino ist gegenüber der Bank e Die erste Straße links und immer geradeaus f Links, erste Straße rechts und erste Straße links. Das Restaurant ist gegenüber der Post g Hier links, rechts und dann immer geradeaus h 3 Kilometer **Revision 1** a Wie komme ich zum Bahnhof? b Ist das weit? c Wo kann ich hier Briefmarken kaufen? d Wo ist hier eine Bank? e Gibt es ein Hotel in der Nähe? f Haben Sie noch Zimmer frei? 2 a die erste Straße rechts b die zweite Straße links c geradeaus d um die Ecke e auf der linken Seite f auf der rechten Seite g ein Einzelzimmer mit Bad h ein Doppelzimmer mit Dusche i mit dem Auto j zu Fuß 3 a Es tut mir Leid b Ich verstehe nicht c Ich weiß es nicht d Entschuldigen Sie, wie bitte? f Vielen Dank **Sign language** a Post office b Bank c Town hall d Cinema e Swimming baths

Unit 10

1 a i b iii c iv d ii 2 a Spielen wir Montagabend Tennis? b Gehen wir morgen Abend ins Kino? c Gehen wir heute um acht Uhr in die Pizzeria? d Gehen wir Mittwochnachmittag schwimmen? e Spielen wir Samstag um elf Uhr Squash? f Gehen wir

Freitagabend ins Restaurant? **3 a** Das geht leider nicht; **b** Wie wäre es mit Donnerstagabend? **4 a** Gut, danke und Ihnen? **b** Am Montag, den 15. Juli **c** Um achtzehn Uhr fünfunddreißig **d** Um halb zehn **e** Bis Freitagabend **f** Um neunzehn Uhr dreißig **g** Um halb acht **h** Auf Wiederhören **Revision 1 a** Montag den zweiten Mai um halb eins **b** Freitag, den 24. Dezember um vierzehn Uhr dreißig **c** nächsten Samstag um Viertel nach elf **d** nächste Woche am Donnerstag um sechzehn Uhr dreißig **e** am Mittwoch den 16. April um Viertel nach neun **f** am Samstag den ersten September um siebzehn Uhr **g** nächsten Dienstag um dreizehn Uhr dreißig **h** am Freitag um acht Uhr **Listening exercise 18 1** Café at eleven tomorrow morning **2** Pub, tomorrow evening at 8.30 **3 15** July at 2pm in Hamburg **4 6** April 8pm (other person's house) **5 24** October 7.30pm (speaker's house) **6 7** August 7.30pm (speaker's house) **7 16.45 9** September at the station. **8 18.35** Friday 14 March at the airport

Unit 11

1 a -e **b** -en **c** -st **d** wir form -en **2 a** er **b** wir **c** sie (plural) **d** Sie (polite) **e** du **f** ich **3 a** holen **b** lernen **c** arbeiten **d** fragen **e** sagen **f** tanzen **4 a** gehört **b** gebraucht **c** geführt **d** gespielt **e** gehabt **f** gekocht **5 a** lesen **b** geben **c** schlafen **d** rufen **e** sehen **f** fahren **g** waschen

Unit 12

1 a mein Vater **b** meine Schwester **c** mein Großvater **d** meine Eltern **e** meine Freundin **f** meine Mutter **g** mein Bruder **h** meine Großmutter **i** meine Frau **j** mein Mann **k** mein Sohn **l** meine Tochter **m** meine Oma **n** mein Opa **o** meine Schwiegermutter **Listening exercise 19 a** Vater Oma Opa Schwester Hund **b** Vater Mutter Sohn Tochter **c** Bruder Schwester Eltern Großeltern Hund **3 a** die Töchter **b** die Tische **c** die Stühle **d** die Häuser **4 a** i/ iv/ v/ vii **b** ii/ iii/ vi **5 a** der

Arbeitsbeginn **b** die Arbeitspause **c** das Arbeitszimmer **d** das Arbeitsende **e** der Arbeitstisch **f** die Arbeitszeit **g** die Arbeitswoche **h** der Arbeitsschluss **i** der Arbeitsvertrag **6 a** das Verkaufsbüro **b** das Informationsbüro **c** das Postamt **d** das Reisebüro **7** Herr Braun says **b c f h i**; Silke says **a d e g j Listening exercise 20 1** Car mechanic for BMW **2** Nurse **3** Business woman **4** Car electrician for a car firm **5** Hairdresser **6** Company rep **7** Business woman (in commerce) **8** Waiter

Unit 13

1 a Elektrogeschäft **b** Supermarkt **c** Kaufhaus **d** Konditorei **e** Bäckerei **f** Metzgerei **g** Fotogeschäft **h** Gemüseladen **i** Drogerie **j** Apotheke **k** Blumengeschäft **l** Zeitungskiosk **m** Tabakhändler **2 a** Film **b** CD/Kassette **c** Briefmarken **d** Zahnpasta **3 a** meine Freundin **b** meinen Bruder **c** meine Großmutter **d** meine Frau **e** meinen Mann **f** meine Mutter **g** meinen Freund **j** meinen Sohn **4 a** Haben Sie …? **i** ein Buch **ii** Schreibpapier **iii** eine Flasche Parfüm **b** Ich suche … **i** eine Flasche Wein **ii** Weingläser **iii** einen Bierkrug **c** Ich möchte … **i** einen Schal **ii** Ohrringe **iii** einen Kuchen **Listening exercise 21 1** book for father **2** winter coat for daughter **3** blue pullover for husband **4** flowers for Frau Fischer **5** cake for Fräulein Sievers **6** toothpaste for self **5 a** Ich möchte einen Pullover, blau Größe 38 **b** eine Bluse, rot, Größe 34 **c** eine Hose, braun, Größe 36 **d** einen Wollschal, grün **e** ein Paar Handschuhe, schwarz **f** ein Hemd, weiß, aus Baumwolle **6 a** Ich möchte einen Schal für meine Mutter **b** blau **c** dunkelblau **d** Aus Wolle? **e** Wie viel kostet er? **f** Das ist zu teuer. Haben Sie etwas Billigeres? **g** Ich nehme ihn **h** Ich möchte ein Paar Handschuhe **i** schwarz, aus Leder **j** Ich weiß es nicht **k** groß **l** Ich nehme sie, könnten Sie sie als Geschenk einpacken? **m** Haben Sie eine Straßenkarte? **n** Wo ist die Buchabteilung? **o** Wo ist der Fahrstuhl?

p Vielen Dank **Listening exercise 22 1** road map of North Germany **2** white shirt size 44 **3** brown corduroy trousers **4** pair of jeans size 38 **5** blue track suit **6** black lycra swimming costume size 40 **7 a** ground floor **b** 4th **c** 3rd **d** 4th **e** ground floor **f** 1st **g** basement **h** 3rd **i** basement **j** 2nd **k** ground floor **l** 1st

Unit 14

1 a Wann kommt der Zug in München an? **b** Wann fährt der Zug ab? **c** Wie schreibt man das? **d** Wie geht es Ihnen? **e** Wo wohnen Sie? **2 a** nach München **b** nach Italien **c** aus England **d** aus London **3 a** Nach Berlin, einmal einfach **b** Einmal nach Salzburg, hin und zurück **c** Dreimal nach Mannheim, hin und zurück **d** Zwei Rückfahrkarten nach Koblenz **e** Zweimal einfach nach Osnabrück **f** Einmal nach Innsbruck, hin und zurück **4 a** Einmal nach Köln bitte, hin und zurück **b** Zweite. Wie viel kostet es? **c** Wann fährt der Zug? **d** Wo fährt er ab? **e** Vielen Dank **f** Wann fährt der nächste Zug nach München? **g** Wie viel kostet es? **h** D-Zug! Muss ich umsteigen? **i** Wann kommt er in München an? **j** Wo fährt er ab? **Listening exercise 23 1 a** Bremen **b** return **c** 14.49 **d** 16.12 **e** no **f** €42,25 **g** 8 **2 a** Cologne **b** return **c** 9.39 **d** 13.48 **e** no **f** €108 **g** 10 **3 a** Vienna **b** single **c** 10.14 **d** 20.53 **e** no **f** €143,50 **g** 9 **5** Ich fliege von Manchester um 11.15 Uhr ab. Ich komme in London um 12.00 Uhr an. Ich fliege ab London um 13.45 Uhr. Ich komme in Hamburg um 14.15 Uhr an. Die Flugnummer ist BA 5377 **6 a** Wann ist der Flug nach Manchester? **b** Ist der Flug direkt? **c** Wie lautet die Flugnummer? **d** Wann komme ich in Manchester an? **7 a** Hallo. Wie geht es dir? **b** Auch gut. **c** Am Sonntag den 26. Oktober. **d** Um 16 Uhr **e** LH 123 Wo treffen wir uns? **f** Ich freue mich schon darauf **g** Tschüss **h** Hallo Wie geht's? **i** Auch gut danke. Wann kommst du? **j** Um wie viel Uhr? Wann landet die Maschine? **k** Wie ist die Flugnummer? **l** Wir treffen uns im Flughafen **m** Bis dann. Tschüss **8 a** um 14.30 in Düsseldorf an **b** um 9.05 in München an **c** um 11.30 in Köln an **d** um 18.35 Uhr in Hamburg an **e** um 21.20 in Wien an **f** um 17.45 in Frankfurt an **Listening exercise 24 1** Tues 21.35 flight LH12 **2** Tues 13.45 BA52 **3** Saturday 10.30 LH25 **4** Thurs 8.15 BA 308 **5** Fri 16th 11.05 LH 207 **6** Weds 14th 15.30 BA 125 **9 a** wolf's castle **b** fish stream **c** new castle **d** Spa Ischl **e** Gelsen churches **f** Ingol town **g** Ammer lake **h** Heather mountain **i** new churches **j** Friedrich's harbour **k** two bridges **l** salt castle **m** Chiem lake **n** Spa town **o** upper village **p** mill village **q** stony stream **r** Magda's castle **s** Osna bridge **t** the Black Forest **u** new town **v** Rhine castle **w** Gunter's village **x** Mann's home

Unit 15

1 a between 6 and 9.30 am **b** between 12 and 2 pm **c** yes (between 6 and 10 am) **d** yes (between 10 am and 6 pm) **2 a** eine Portion Pommes **b** zwei Bratwürste **c** Bockwurst und Pommes zweimal **d** eine Dose Cola **e** ein Bier **f** zwei Waffeln **Listening exercise 25 1** Sausage with potato salad and portion chips **2** Waffles with hot cherry sauce **3** 2 Curry sausage and potato purée **4** Frankfurter, mustard and bread roll **5** Reibekuchen (potato fritter) with apple sauce **6** Chips **7** 1 ham sandwich and 1 cheese sandwich **8** 2 beers and a coke **3 a** Ich möchte einmal Bratwurst mit Pommes **b** Ketchup **c** Ja, eine Currywurst mit Kartoffelsalat **d** Eine Cola und ein Bier. Das ist alles. Was macht das? **e** So. 50 Euros **f** Ja, ich habe zwei Euro **4 a** ii **b** i **c** iv **d** vii **e** v and vi **f** iii **5 a** Haben Sie …? ein Messer; ein Glas; einen Löffel; einen Teller **b** Salz; Ketchup; Senf; Zucker; Brot **6 a** Bitte! **b** Ich brauche noch einen Teller **c** Haben Sie Salz? **d** Haben Sie Ketchup? **e** Nein, danke das ist alles **f** Fräulein **g** Noch ein Glas bitte **h** Haben Sie OK

Sauce? i Noch ein Bier und ein Glas Limonade 7 a Taschenmesser b Küchenmesser c Brotmesser 8 a €1,30 b €2,40 c €1,80 d €1,30 e €1,65 f €1,20 g €1,85 h €1,15 i €3,25 j €2,95

Unit 16

Listening exercise 26 1 Wienerschnitzel, chips, lettuce **2** Chicken, chips and tomato salad **3** Roast pork with mashed potatoes and sour pickled cabbage **4** Trout, boiled potatoes and red cabbage **5** Pork fillet, rice and asparagus **6** Jägerschnitzel (escalope) with noodles and beans **1** Magst du…?/Isst du gern…?/Trinkst du gern…? a Fleisch b Fisch c Bier d Tee mit Milch e Tee mit Zitrone f Kuchen **2** Ist hier frei? b Was ist die Tagessuppe? c Haben Sie Tomatensuppe? d Ich möchte … e Nein. Das schmeckt mir nicht f Ich nehme … g mit … h und zu trinken … i Was empfehlen Sie? j Ich nehme das k Ja, mit Sahne l Ja, bitte **3** a Do you want something to drink with it? b Do you want a dessert? c Which flavour? d Do you want ketchup? e Did you like it? f Together or separately?

Unit 17

1 a Gehen Sie gern ins Kino? b Tanzen Sie gern c Gehen Sie gern schwimmen? d Spielen Sie gern Karten? e Fahren Sie gern Rad? f Sehen Sie gern fern? **2** a Spielst du gern Squash? b Spielst du gern Fußball? c Läufst du gern Ski? d Spielst du gern Tennis? e Fährst du gern Rad? f Spielst du gern Schach? **3** a Ich spiele gern Tennis b Ich spiele gern Fußball c Ich fahre gern Rad d Ich gehe gern klettern e Ich spiele gern Karten f Ich spiele gern Golf

Listening exercise 27

Like	Dislike
1 swimming	dancing
2 tennis/badminton	table tennis
3 walking	jogging
4 swimming/reading	football

5 football
6 skiing/bike
4 a Morgen Vormittag spiele ich Tennis. Kommen Sie mit? b Morgen Abend gehen wir schwimmen. Kommen Sie mit? c Heute Abend spielen wir Karten. Haben Sie Lust Karten zu spielen? d Heute Nachmittag gehen wir angeln. Kommen Sie mit? e Heute Abend gehen wir in ein Nachtlokal. Kommen Sie mit? f Samstagnachmittag gehen wir zum Fußball. g Kommen Sie mit? h Das Spiel beginnt um … i Haben Sie Lust danach Tennis zu spielen? **5** a Ja, gerne. Um wie viel Uhr? b Wo treffen wir uns? c Nein. Ich habe keine Lust. Ich spiele lieber Tennis d Um wie viel Uhr? e Wo treffen wir uns? f Gerne. Ich bin noch nie Ski gefahren g Um wie viel Uhr? h Wann kommen wir zurück? i Gut. Ich freue mich schon darauf **6** golf-minigolf, sand yachting, table tennis, volleyball, chess, bowling, fishing, surfing, woodland fitness circuit, cycling, swimming, tennis, sailing **7** a i / iv / v / vii / ix b ii / iii / vi / viii / x **Listening exercise 28 1** playing cards **2** cycling **3** watching TV **4** reading books **5** jogging **6** swimming **7** skiing **8** cinema **8** a Schneemann b Schneeball c Schneeballschlacht d Schneeflocken e Schneeglöckchen f Schneeketten g Schneebrille h Schneeraupe i Schneesturm

Unit 18

Listening exercise 29 1 fill up with super plus **2** 20 litres of diesel **3** check the tyre pressures **4** Do you take credit cards? **5** clean the windscreen **6** Where is the cash desk? **1** Können wir …? i den Reifendruck prüfen ii die Windschutzscheibe putzen iii den Ölstand prüfen **2** a iii b v c i d vi e ii f iv **3** Ich bin auf … a der A4 zwischen Köln und Aachen Richtung Aachen b der A1 in der Nähe von Solingen Richtung Dortmund c der A5, in der Nähe von Offenburg Richtung Basel d der A8 in der Nähe von Augsburg Richtung München e der B10 in der Nähe von Geislingen, zwischen Stuttgart und Ulm, Richtung Ulm **Listening exercise 30** near Hannover, near Munich and near Berlin **4** a near Friedberg **b** because of an accident **c** at Augsburg **d** the B2 **5** **a** What is wrong? **b** What sort of car you have **c** Where you are **d** The make of your car **e** If you are a member of an automobile club **Listening exercise 31** **1** breakdown **2** broken windscreen **3** run out of petrol **4** puncture **5** no water and overheating **6** won't start **7** Light not working; can you change the bulb? **6 a** Wo kann ich parken? **b** Wie komme ich zum Bahnhof? **c** Wo kann ich hier parken? Der Parkplatz ist voll **d** Wo ist die Tiefgarage? **e** Ist es teuer? **f** Und nach 8.00 Uhr? **g** Haben Sie Kleingeld? **h** zwei fünfzig Cent Münzen **7 a** lorries **b** cars

Unit 19

1 a Ich habe eine Erkältung **b** Ich fühle mich nicht wohl **c** Haben Sie etwas gegen einen Sonnenbrand? **d** Wie oft soll ich sie einnehmen? **e** Ich habe Husten **f** Ich habe Zahnschmerzen **Listening exercise 32** **1** headache **2** flu **3** temperature and sore throat **4** cold **2 a** Ich fühle mich nicht wohl **b** Ich habe Fieber, Kopfschmerzen und Halsschmerzen **c** Haben Sie etwas gegen Kopfschmerzen? **3 a** iii **b** ii **c** vi **d** v **e** iv **f** i **4 a** 8.30–1 and 2.15–6 **b** 8.30–1 and 2.15–4 **c** no **6 a** Gibt es eine Apotheke in der Nähe? **b** Wann ist sie offen? **c** Bis wann? **7 a** Monday to Friday 8.45 to 18.30 and on Saturday 8.45 till 1pm except on the first Saturday of the month when it stays open till 6pm **b** Works holiday from 14 to 28 July

Unit 20

1 a iii **b** v **c** i **d** ii **e** iv **Listening exercise 33** **1** send a photo **2** read e-mails **3** save a document **4** book a flight **5** send an email **6** surf the internet **7** look up train times **8** download a town plan

Unit 21

1 vacancies; full; accommodation listing **2** 1/m, 2/f, 3/b, 4/k, 5/a, 6/g, 7/p, 8/d, 9/c, 10/e, 11/h, 12/n, 13/j, 14/i, 15/o, 16/l **3** i e, ii a, iii h, iv g, v c, vi b, vii d, viii f **4 a** Wie komme ich am besten zur Messe? **b** Welche Buslinie? **c** Wie oft fährt sie? **d** Welche U-Bahn? **e** Muss ich umsteigen? **f** Wie oft fährt sie? **g** Vielen Dank **h** eine Eintrittskarte **i** Einkäufer **j** ... **5 a** Wir brauchen einen Schlüssel für den Stand **b** einundzwanzig **c** Wir haben keinen Strom **d** Wo bekommt man Aschenbecher? **e** Wo bekommt man Wasser **6 a** no cycling **b** do not enter the building site **c** do not walk on the grass **d** beware of traffic from the right **e** no smoking, **f** use the opposite pavement **g** beware of level crossing **h** no entry **Listening exercise 34** **1** in the office on the 7th floor **2** in the restaurant here on the 2nd floor **3** snack bars everywhere, one in each exhibition hall **4** in the corner: men on left, women on right **5** in the entrance hall **6 a** viii **b** iv **c** v **d** vii **e** i **f** ii **g** iii **h** vi **i** ix

grammar summary

Nouns and articles ('the' and 'a')

In German all nouns are either masculine, feminine or neuter.
The words for *the* and *a* change according to the gender of the
noun.

The definite article ('the')

The word for *the* with | masculine words is | **der** (der Mann)
| feminine | **die** (die Frau)
| neuter | **das** (das Buch)

The indefinite article ('a')

The word for *a* with | masculine words is | **ein** (ein Mann)
| feminine | **eine** (eine Frau)
| neuter | **ein** (ein Buch)

For more details see Unit 8 page 74.

Kein ('not a')

This is a negative form of the indefinite article which we do
not have in English.

Masc:	Ich habe keinen Stuhl.	*I haven't a chair.*
Fem:	Ich habe keine Zeit.	*I haven't time.*
Neut:	ich habe kein Auto.	*I haven't a car.*

Plurals

For information about the plural forms see Unit 12 page 117.

Masculine nouns

The masculine forms **der/ein/kein** change to **den/einen/keinen** when they are used with the object of the sentence.

Der Hund   *but* Ich habe **einen** Hund. (*I have a dog*)
Ein Teller   *but* Ich brauche **einen** Teller. (*I need a plate*)
Kein Mantel   *but* Sie hat **keinen** Mantel. (*She hasn't a coat*)

For some examples see Unit 13 page 130 and Unit 15 page 150.

Nouns and trigger words (prepositions)

Some words (e.g. **mit**, *with*; **zu**, *to*) act as trigger words and change **der** to **dem**, **die** to **der**, **das** to **dem**, and **die** (plural) to **den**. For more information see Unit 8 pages 77–8, Unit 9 page 81 and Unit 17 page 173.

These words are always trigger words:

aus	*from/out of*	aus dem Schrank *from the cupboard*
bei	*at/near*	bei der Post *at the post office*
gegenüber	*opposite*	gegenüber dem Café *opposite the café*
mit	*with*	mit dem Bus *with/by bus*
nach	*after*	nach der Pause *after the break*
zu	*to*	zu der Bank *to the bank*

These words are usually trigger words:

an	*on*	an der Hauptstraße *on the main street*
auf	*on*	auf dem Tisch *on the table*
in	*in*	im Kaufhaus *in the store*

Personal pronouns

Singular		Plural	
ich	*I*	**wir**	*we*
du	*you*	**ihr**	*you*
er	*he*	**sie**	*they*
sie	*she*	**Sie**	*you (polite form)*
es	*it*		

		Other forms			
	Singular			**Plural**	
mich	me	**mir**	to me	**uns**	us/to us
dich	you	**dir**	to you	**euch**	you/to you
ihn	him	**ihm**	to him	**sie**	them
sie	her	**ihr**	to her	**Sie**	you
es	it	**ihm**	to it	**ihnen**	to them
				Ihnen	to you

For more information about the different words for *you* see Unit 4, pages 34–5.

Table of irregular verbs

Infinitive	He/she	Past (imp.)	Past (perf.)	English
*an/rufen	ruft/an	rief/an	habe angerufen	*to ring up*
*auf/stehen	steht/auf	stand/auf	bin aufgestanden	*to get up*
*-bleiben	bleibt	blieb	bin geblieben	*to stay/ remain*
essen	isst	aß	habe gegessen	*to eat*
*-fahren	fährt	fuhr	bin gefahren	*to go/drive*
*-fliegen	fliegt	flog	bin geflogen	*to fly*
(*)geben	gibt	gab	habe gegeben	*to give*
*gehen	geht	ging	bin gegangen	*to go/walk*
haben	hat	hatte	habe gehabt	*to have*
*kommen	kommt	kam	bin gekommen	*to come*
*laufen	läuft	lief	bin gelaufen	*to run*
lesen	liest	las	habe gelesen	*to read*
nehmen	nimmt	nahm	habe genommen	*to take*
schlafen	schläft	schlief	habe geschlafen	*to sleep*
schreiben	schreibt	schrieb	habe geschrieben	*to write*
*schwimmen	schwimmt	schwamm	bin geschwommen	*to swim*
sehen	sieht	sah	habe gesehen	*to see*
sein	ist	war	bin gewesen	*to be*
sprechen	spricht	sprach	habe gesprochen	*to speak*
tragen	trägt	trug	habe getragen	*to wear/ carry*
trinken	trinkt	trank	habe getrunken	*to drink*
verlieren	verliert	verlor	habe verloren	*to lose*
wissen	weiß	wusste	habe gewusst	*to know*
ziehen	zieht	zog	habe gezogen	*to pull*

... and two regular ones

machen	macht	machte	habe gemacht	*to make*
spielen	spielt	spielte	habe gespielt	*to play*

For more information about verbs see Unit 11, and about separable verbs see Unit 17.

English–German vocabulary

* this word is sometimes a trigger word (page 219)
** this word is always a trigger word
Numbers are page references

after nach**, **62**
(this) afternoon (heute) Nachmittag, **170**
also auch
always immer
(I) am (ich) bin, **111**
and und
are sind, **111**
between zwischen*

big groß
Bill, please Zahlen, bitte, **163**

Can you? Kannst du?/Können Sie?
cheap billig
child das Kind
colour die Farbe, **131**

daughter die Tochter
day der Tag
difficult/hard schwer/schwierig
to do machen

(this) evening (heute) Abend
every day jeden Tag
Excuse me Entschuldigen Sie, bitte
expensive teuer

far weit
fast schnell

for für
I am looking forward to it Ich freue mich darauf
friend der Freund/die Freundin
in front of vor*

girl das Mädchen
to go (on foot) gehen; *to go (travel)* fahren
good gut

(he) has (er) hat, **111**
to have haben, **111**
(I) have (ich) habe; *Have you ...?* Haben Sie ...?; *I haven't a ...* Ich habe kein/e/en...
he er
her ihr/e
him ihn
his sein/e
(in the) holidays (in den) Ferien
How? Wie?; How many? Wie viele?

I ich
in in*, **173**
is ist

to live wohnen

May I? Darf ich?
me mich

to *meet* treffen
Mr Herr
Mrs Frau
my mein/e

near neben*
new neu
nice schön
no nein

on an*/auf*, **66, 90, 173**
old alt
opposite gegenüber, **90**

Pardon? Wie bitte?
please bitte
possible möglich

quite ganz

it's raining es regnet
room das Zimmer

she sie
short kurz
slow langsam
small klein
sometimes ab und zu/manchmal
son der Sohn
I'm sorry Es tut mir Leid

thank you danke/vielen Dank
their ihr/e
there is/there are es gibt
they/them sie/sie
tired müde
to zu**, **62, 81, 173**
today heute
tomorrow morgen

too zu

until bis

I was ich war
week die Woche
with mit*, **90**
without ohne
I would like ich möchte
to write schreiben

yes ja
yesterday gestern
young jung
you (see Unit 4 pages **34–5**)

* this word is sometimes a trigger word
** this is always a trigger word (der→dem/das→dem/die→der)
Numbers are page references

Remember:

der tells you a word is a masculine word;
die tells you a word is a feminine word;
das tells you a word is a neuter word.

der Abend *evening*
abends *in the evening*
alt *old*
am ... (an + dem) *on the...*, **66, 173**
an* *on*, **94**
an/rufen *to call, phone*; ich rufe ... an *I'll ring ...*, **83**
der Anzug *suit*
die Anschrift *address*, **47**
auch *also*
auf* *on*: auf der rechten/linken Seite *on the right/left side*, **82**; auf Wiedersehen *goodbye*
aus** *from/out of*
die Auskunft *information*
das Ausland *abroad*
die Aussicht *view*
der Ausweis *identity card*, **47**
die Autobahn *motorway*

das Bad *bath*
der Bahnhof *station*
bei** *at/near*, **182**

der Beruf *job*
besetzt *engaged*
besuchen *to visit*; ich besuche *I visit*
die Bibliothek *library*, **72**
der Biergarten *beer garden*, **76**
billig *cheap*
ich bin *I am*, **111**
der Bindestrich *hyphen*, **37**
bitte *please*; Wie bitte? *Pardon?*
Bitte schön *Here you are*
bleiben *to stay or remain*; ich bleibe *I stay*
brauchen *to need*; ich brauche *I need*
der Brief *letter*
die Briefmarke *postage stamp*
die Brücke *bridge*, **72**
der Buchstabe *letter (of the alphabet)*
die Bushaltestelle *bus stop*

der Campingplatz *campsite*

da *there*
Damen *ladies*
Danke/Dankeschön *thank you*
dann *then*
das tut mir Leid *I'm sorry*
der Dom *cathedral*, **72**
das Doppelbett *double bed*
das Doppelzimmer *double room*,
  52
dort drüben *over there*, **73**
die Dose *tin/can*, **148**
drücken *to press/push*; ich
  drücke *I press*
dunkel *dark*
durch *through*
dürfen *to be allowed to*; ich darf
  I may
die Dusche *shower*

die Einladung *invitation*, **95**
das Einzelzimmer *single room*,
  52
der Empfangstisch *reception
  desk*
Entschuldigen Sie, bitte *Excuse
  me, please*
er *he*
erst/e *the first*; am ersten *on the
  first*
es *it*; Es geht mir gut *I am well*
essen *to eat*
etwas *some*

fahren *to drive*; ich fahre *I drive*
der Fahrstuhl *lift*
die Familie *family*
die Farbe *colour*
die Feiertage *holidays*, **92**
das Fenster *window*
der Fernseher *television*
die Flasche *bottle*
der Flughafen *airport*, **141**
die Frau *woman/wife/Mrs*
das Fräulein *young lady/Miss*
frei *free*
das Freibad *open-air swimming
  pool*, **72**
Ich freue mich ... *I am looking
  forward ...*
das Frühstück *breakfast*
für *for*

zu Fuß *on foot*, **83**

ganz *quite*
der Geburtstag *birthday*
gegenüber *opposite*, **90**
gehen *to go*; ich gehe *I go*; Geht
  das? *Is that all right?*; Es geht
  It's all right
genau *exactly*
geradeaus *straight ahead*, **82**
gern/e *willingly/with pleasure*,
  95, 161
das Geschenk *present*
geschlossen *closed*, **192**
gestern *yesterday*
gesund *healthy*
gleich *immediately/straight away*
groß *big*
die Größe *size*
gut *good/well*

haben *to have*, **111**: Haben
  Sie...? *Have you ...?*
halb *half*, **64**
Haupt- *main*; Hauptbahnhof
  main station
heiß *hot*
heißen *to be called*; ich heiße
  I am called
der Herr *man/Mr/husband*; die
  Herren *men*
heute *today*, **170**
hier *here*
holen *to fetch*; ich hole *I fetch*,
  105, 169

ich *I*
immer *always*
inbegriffen *included*
das Inland *inland*

ja *yes*; jawohl *yes indeed*
die Jugendherberge *youth hostel*

kalt *cold*
kaputt *broken*
kaufen *to buy*; ich kaufe *I buy*
kein/e *not a*
Ich habe kein/e/en ... *I haven't
  a ...*
der Kellner *waiter*
das Kino *cinema*, **72**

die Kirche *church*, **72**
klein *small*
die Kneipe *pub*, **72**
kommen *to come*; ich komme *I come*
Kopfschmerzen (pl.) *headache*, **194**
krank *ill*, **194**
das Krankenhaus *hospital*, **72**

langsam *slow*; lamgsamer *slower*
laut *loud/noisy*
ledig *unmarried*, **47**
leider *unfortunately*
lieber *rather*; ich trinke lieber Tee *I would prefer tea*
links *left*

machen *to make*; ich mache *I make*, **103**
der Mann *husband*
die Milch *milk*
mit** *with*, **90**
ich möchte *I would like*, **54–5**, **59**
morgen *tomorrow*, **174**
müde *tired*

nach** *after/past*, **62**
nächst/e *next*, **139**
die Nacht *night*
nehmen *to take*; ich nehme *I take*, **131**
nicht *not*
noch *still/yet/more*
nur *only*

oder *or*
ohne *without*
Ostern *Easter*, **95**

die Polizei *police*
die Postleitzahl *postcode*, **43**
prima! *great!*, **97**

die Quittung *receipt*

das Rathaus *town hall*, **72**
rechts *right*
die Reise *journey*
die Rolltreppe *escalator*

rot *red*

das Schloss *castle*
der Schlüssel *key*
schnell *quick/fast*
schwimmen *to swim*; ich schwimme *I swim*
sehen *to see*; ich sehe *I see*
sehr *very*
seit** *since*
sie *she/they*; Sie *you*, **103**
sind *are*; sein, **111** *to be*; Sind Sie …? *Are you …?*
spielen *to play*; ich spiele *I play*
sprechen *to speak*, ich spreche *I speak*
die Straße *street*, **72**
das Stück *piece*
süß *sweet*

die Tankstelle *petrol station*, **178**
die Telefonauskunft *directory inquiries*
teuer *expensive*
treffen *to meet*; Treffen wir uns? *Shall we meet?*, **66**
trinken *to drink*; ich trinke *I drink*
trocken *dry*
Tschüs/Tschüss *bye*

die Uhr *clock*, **62**
um *at/around*, **66**

verboten *forbidden*
verheiratet *married*
verlieren *to lose*; verloren *lost*
verstehen *to understand*; ich verstehe *I understand*
viel/e *many*; vielen Dank *many thanks*
Viertel *quarter*, **62**
von** *of/from*, **94**
vor* *before/to*, **62**
die Vorwahl *(telephone) code*, **43**

wählen *to dial/to choose*, **43**
Wann? *When?*
Was? *What?*; Was für …? *What*

kind of ...?
der Wecker *alarm clock*, **69**
weiß *white*
ich weiß *I know*
Weihnachten *Christmas*
weit *far*
Welche/r? *Which?*
Wer? *Who?*
Wie? *How?*; Wie bitte?
  Pardon?; Wie viele? *How
  many?*
Wiederholen Sie, bitte *Please
  repeat*
Wo? *Where?*
die Woche *week*, **97**
wohnen *to live*; ich wohne *I live*

zahlen *to pay*; Zahlen, bitte!
  Bill please!, **163**
die Zeit *time*
ziemlich *rather*
das Zimmer *room*
zu** *to*, **81, 173**; zu *too*, **57**
der Zucker *sugar*
zuerst *at first*
der Zug *train*; mit dem Zug *by
  train*
zwischen *between*, **179**